MIDDLE KINGDOM

Legendary Beginning of China and the Bible

By

Ken Kwok

Middle Kingdom
Legendary Beginning of China and the Bible

Copyright © 2008 Ken Kwok
Cover photo by Corrine Leung

All rights reserved

ISBN: 978-0-557-00325-9

No part of this book may be reproduced or transmitted in any form or by any means electronic or mechanical, including photocopying and recording, or by any information storage and retrieval system, without the written permission from the publisher.

Scripture quotations from New International Version Bible and the King James Version Bible

This book is dedicated to God who gives me the courage and strength to face adversity. I am indebted to Corrine, my eternal love and baby; my dearest dad and mom who did their best to raise ten children; Dana and Susanna, my sisters who sacrificed a lot for my family; Lawrence, my virtuous brother; Yung Kai Sing, my righteous cousin; and the following people whom I am grateful for their friendship: Sidney Chan, Happie So, Simon Yan, Ryan and Tony Kim, Robert Gibson, Charles Atkinson, Kan Chan and; the gracious folks (1993-1995) of Faith Baptist Church in Vancouver where my wife and I got baptized.

Contents

Introduction 4
Chapter 1 Biblical Migration 15
Chapter 2 Ancient Messengers of Yahweh to China 24
Chapter 3 The East. 34
Chapter 4 The First Chinese People 38
Chapter 5 Son of Heaven 52
Chapter 6 Vanished Mongoloid Race. 66
Chapter 7 Tower of Babel 77
Chapter 8 Sages. 85
Chapter 9 Primitive Chinese People 98
Chapter 10 Shang-Ti. 105
Chapter 11 Virtuous Emperor. 113
Chapter 12 Shang from Shem. 122
Chapter 13 Han from Ham. 134
Chapter 14 Caucasian from Japheth 144
Chapter 15 Chinese Character 149
Suggested Timeline 157
General References 158

INTRODUCTION

IN AD 635, ALUOBEN, a Persian bishop, from the Assyrian Church of the East and his entourage arrived in Chang An (Xian), the capital of the Tang Dynasty. They were warmly welcome by Emperor Taizong. Aluoben presented the Christian Gospel to the emperor and won his favor and reverence. Immediately, Aluoben was commissioned to translate the gospel for the Chinese people. For the next 200 years Nestorian Christianity mixed with Taoist and Buddhist messages was spread all over China. Hundreds of Christian temples were erected. This rising new religion in Tang China was called the "Luminous Religion". Their eastern and western philosophies entwined Gospel was successfully evangelized to the Chinese people and won many followers.

Unfortunately by AD 845, the renaissance of Confucianism had led to the persecution of the Luminous followers and the ultimate destruction of their existence in China. Many centuries passed after the great persecution, the Luminous Religion and its Christian based evangelism were totally forgotten in China.

A Stone Sutra Stele dated AD 781 was unearthed in a grave site by accident in AD 1625 in Xian. It recounted the major events and teachings of the Luminous Religion which began in AD 635 during the

Tang Dynasty. On top of the stone stele was a small cross fended by two dragons. There is no doubt the symbol is the Christian cross. The Stone Sutra Stele is now displayed in the Forest of Stone Stele Museum in Xian.

Despite the Stone Sutra Stele has been unearthed for centuries, no one in China has any interest in researching and finding out the background of events recounted on the stele. If not because of the devoted research of Martin Palmer, author of the book "The Jesus Sutra" and a passionate westerner in Chinese culture, the religious and cultural significance of the Stone Sutra Stele will never be known to the world.

Chinese people including me myself are not aware of Christianity had entered China in such an early date in the past. In fact, I think Chinese people have no idea that Christianity had thrived in China for 200 years during the Tang Dynasty (AD 618-907)! Believers of Christ had arrived in China in the 5th Century much earlier than most people think of the first Christian missionary by Jesuit Matteo Ricci who arrived in China in AD 1601. Early Christian impact to the Chinese world was not deep until the arrival of Aluoben in AD 635. Thereafter, Christianity was widespread in all of Tang China for 200 years. But even this profound impact of Christianity in China had a short lived memory in the mind of Chinese people. The ancient Chinese world was like a pot of steaming and delicious soup boiled with all kinds of enhancing ingredients but all Chinese people could remember was the taste.

What if the same event had happened way back in the beginning time of China? What if the believers of Yahweh from the line of Seth and Shem had reached pre-dynastic China and spread the knowledge of God and the early stories in the Book of Genesis to early Chinese people? Could this be how people in the legendary history of China possess knowledge of a supreme god called Shang-Ti, kingdom of heaven, and the mandate of heaven?

Much like the fate of the Luminous Religion which ended in total oblivion, the believers of Yahweh from the line of Seth and Shem in China were totally forgotten and their faith gradually eroded into obscurity.

I believe some ancient migrants [early settlers] in pre-dynastic China were from the line of Seth and Shem. They were steadfast believers and messengers of Yahweh in everywhere they went. They were the ones who seeded China with the knowledge of monotheism and the early stories in the Book of Genesis. They were part of the population in the legendary beginning of China. Their teaching of love, righteousness, and morality to early Chinese people was invaluable but gone unnoticed and forgotten. They were the source of inspiration where virtuous emperors appeared in the still untamed world of pre-dynastic China.

The beginning history of China is shrouded in legends. The time where the legendary history happened was even sketchy (see Suggested Timeline in Appendix). There is no solid archaeological evidence of the existence of Yellow Emperor (around 2800 BC) and the Xia Dynasty (2205 BC to 1766 BC) which was regarded as the earliest tribal dynasty in China. There is still debate whether Yellow Emperor is a fictitious or real historical figure. However, to the majority of Chinese people in China, they believe they are the proud descendants of Yellow Emperor.

Before Yellow Emperor appeared, Chinese legends said a handful of sages appeared out of nowhere separately over an unknown period of time to teach the primitive Chinese people to become more civilized. Who were these mysterious sages? Where did they come from? And how did they become wiser than their own primitive fellowmen?

If the sages were children from the primitive Chinese people, they must be born prodigies. Chinese people must be grateful for the timely miracles of their appearance to help their primitive ancestors transformed into a civilized people.

If the sages were not born from the primitive Chinese people, then they had to come from a higher culture outside of China where they had acquired their knowledge.

There is simply no third alternative to the origin of the sages. They were either a born genius or a foreign genius. There is no way that a primitive people could reinvent themselves by begot prodigies to civilize their own people.

Mankind's first civilization arose in ancient Near East. The Sumerians were the first people to spread civilization to the world. The legendary sages in China could come from people in the ancient Near East.

Up to now archaeologists could only find archaeological evidences of the Shang Dynasty (1766 BC to 1050 BC) in Anyang (Shang palace) and other sites in northeastern China. Thus, the Shang Dynasty marked the beginning point of substantiated Chinese history. However, this doesn't mean the legendary sages, Yellow Emperor, and the Xia Dynasty is fiction. There are ancient Chinese documents made references to their existence. Therefore, Chinese historians included them as legends in the beginning history of China. The truth is the origin of Chinese people is a complicated conundrum.

Chinese historians assumed Mongoloid people were the only type of people occupied China right from the beginning with no intrusion of other races from the outside world. Therefore, all legendary figures such as Yellow Emperor, the three sovereigns, five sages, and the primitive people in Chinese legends were Mongoloid people. Although Chinese archaeologists discovered ancient human skulls and remains that anatomically pointed to the Mongoloid type of human, how could Chinese historians and archaeologists be so sure that Mongoloid people was the only race occupied in China since the dawn of Chinese history?

Right from the beginning, early Chinese people saw the West was the utopia world where eternal happiness existed. Without any particular religion influenced the mind of the early Chinese people, they mysteriously possessed the idea of an utopia paradise in the west (Garden of Eden), a supreme deity (God) ruling heaven and earth, a heavenly empire (Kingdom of God) in the sky, and the obedience to the mandate of heaven (Will of God). How did early people in China invent such profound concepts without any religion? The truth is they didn't.

The above concepts of the early Chinese people suggested that they had a forgotten past in the land of the Bible. I believe some of the children from the line of Seth and Shem as mentioned in the genealogy in Genesis 5:1-32 and 11:10-26 had reached antediluvian and postdiluvian China. Who else would know these things better than the believers of Yahweh who came from the biblical land?

This book is about the believers of Yahweh from the line of Seth and Shem who came to China before or during the legendary historical period of China. The other sons and daughters from the line of Seth in 5:1-32 were one of the ancestors of early tribes in the antediluvian China. Unfortunately, the Deluge sent down by God destroyed all mankind, thus, evidences of their existence were all wiped out from the face of China.

After the Deluge, Noah and his three sons: Shem, Japheth and Ham repopulated the world. They became the second wave of migrants and ancestors in the postdiluvian China. Children from the line of Shem were faithful believers of Yahweh. They were the ones who spread the knowledge of God and the stories happened in the early chapters in the Book of Genesis.

The Bible tells us mankind began in the Garden of Eden somewhere in ancient Iraq. From there mankind dispersed all over the world. As Christian we don't doubt or refute this truth because we believe every word right from the beginning story of the Bible. There is no compromise-period.

To Christians, the origin of mankind is a biblical origin. No amount of scientific and archaeological evidences could change this truth. Christians must either accept the creation of man as is in the Bible or change their religion. This book leans on the truth of the Bible that mankind spread all over the world from the biblical land. Chinese Christians must believe the earliest ancestors of Chinese people came from the biblical land where mankind begun. It is biblical truth which Christians must stop shuffle under the carpet anymore.

I am shocked by some of my Christian friends who believe Darwin's evolution theory that mankind was evolved from apes. How could they be so confused? Did God create Adam an ape or a man? How could these people still think they're a Christian when they compromised the truth of the Bible?

Thanks to Darwin's evolution theory, China promoted Chinese people was evolved from the *Peking Man* (dated 500,000-700,000 years ago) where which archaeologist unearthed in Zhoukoudian near Beijing in 1929. Chinese people were told mankind was evolved from ape. However, Chinese archaeologists forgot to explain which kind of ape did the Chinese evolve from: was it Mongoloid, Caucasian or Negro ape? Had anyone thought why apes in China evolved into Mongoloid Chinese only and not Caucasian or Negro?

Darwin's evolutionary theory is a radical western idea. It is ironic that China has such alacrity to embrace Darwin theory without her normal harsh and belligerent scrutiny of western ideas.

This book explores the obscure footprints left behind by the believers of Yahweh who had migrated to antediluvian and postdiluvian China. They were the other sons and daughters from the line of Seth and Shem mentioned in the genealogy in Genesis 5:1-32 and 11:10-26. They and their descendants were the ones who spread and passed down the stories of Genesis creation, Adam and Eve, Garden of Eden, Satan, the Deluge, Tower of Babel, and the idea of monotheism to the early people in China. This was how early Chinese people possessed the knowledge of a supreme deity called Shang-Ti, the heavenly empire (Heaven), and the mandate of heaven (the Will of God).

The impact of the migrated other children from the line of Seth and Shem to the antediluvian and postdiluvian China had instilled the mind of early Chinese people with the idea of virtue, righteousness, and love for one another. Their spreading of a loving and righteous God had raised the level of moral awareness and social decorum in early Chinese society.

Great figures such as Yellow Emperor was a righteous warrior king and the three renowned emperor Yao, Shun, and Yu were benevolent emperors in the legendary history of China. They possessed extraordinary character of virtue and righteousness. How could they become the paragon of exceptional virtuous men in a still untamed world of barbarism and lawlessness in prehistoric China? Were they born with special noble genes of morality or were they influenced by the children from the line of Shem who spread their faith of a loving and righteous God?

The Bible tells us mankind is originated from ancient Near East. Adam and Eve were the first human couple. Their descendants diverse into three types of races: Negro, Caucasian, and Mongoloid. I believe majority of the Mongoloid people had departed the biblical land and journeyed to the East long before the authors of the Bible could trace them. Mongoloid people dominated East Asia. Due to long isolation from the rest of the world by mountainous terrains and deserts, their posterity had totally forgotten their biblical origin. This book hopes to reconnect them to the divine heritage of the Bible.

The theory presented in this book is my personal opinion. This is my personal quest for revelation of the origin of Chinese people from God. Reader should read this book with an open mind.

After I converted to Christian in 1993, I was extremely curious to know the biblical origin of Chinese people. My urge to find an answer to this question became very personal and very addictive. Since then researching and writing about this topic became my personal mission.

It took me many years to write and rewrite this book. By the time I completed this book, I was exhausted after many years of struggling with long hours of writing, rewriting, research, and finding means to put food on the table. I am grateful to God for sustaining my will to keep me writing.

I pray that this book can arouse the interest of Christians and non-Christians in all over the world to search the Bible as a credible source for the origin of their ancestors where Chinese people also share the divine heritage of the Bible.

Although this book will not proves the migrated children from the line of Seth and Shem had reached early China by scientific or archaeological evidences, the author will let the reader determines if he or she agrees with the things said in this book. Agreement or disagreement is not important; what is importance is Christians must have an open and tolerant mind to freedom of idea and speech.

Even though this book is completed, however, my research for more evidences in this subject continues. I welcome readers to contact me by email: kenkwok@telus.net if you wish to share your thought in this subject with me. I hope you enjoy reading this book as much as I enjoy writing it.

CHAPTER 1 – BIBLICAL MIGRATION

THE BEGINNING CHAPTER OF THE BOOK OF GENESIS tells us God created Adam and Eve, the first human couple, on the sixth day in ancient Near East. Then in Genesis 1:28, God blessed mankind to multiply, rule and fill the earth. The children of Adam and Eve were destined to migrate to other lands in order to fulfill God's blessing. The peopling of the world began before Adam and Eve committed the original sin and continued after they were expelled to the east of Eden.

East was an unknown region waiting for humans to explore. Ancient wanderers heading eastward from ancient Near East could reach the land of prehistoric China in their eastward journey.

By the time of Cain and Abel, mankind had crossed the threshold of the Neolithic Age. Abel was a shepherd and Cain was an agriculturalist. The knowledge of domestication of sheep and the planting of crops had been mastered by man. If you asked me when did the Fall of Adam and Eve happen? I would say it happened between 12000 to 9000 BC where mankind had transformed from hunter gatherers to sedentary farmers and collective dwellers. The appearance of Cain and Abel in the Bible marked mankind entered the world of the knowledge of good and evil.

Cain was banished by God to exile for the rest of his life after he killed Abel. God gave Adam and Eve another son, Seth, to replace Abel. To everyone surprise, the first murderer of mankind suddenly possessed the knowledge of city building. Cain built mankind's first city which he named after his son Enoch. Clearly, the Neolithic era had arrived with the sudden burst of knowledge to mankind through Cain. Therefore, people in the time of Cain and Seth had mastered sufficient skills to equip themselves for migration to distant land such as China in the farthest region in the East.

Before the Deluge, children from the line of Seth and Cain were the first wave of migrants to wander into prehistoric China. Jabal, one of Cain's seventh generation grandchildren was the inventor of tent and the domestication of cattle. His children were more than qualified to wander afar to distant land.

Children from the line of Seth had also reached China. They had smaller number than the people from the line of Cain, thus, their influence on the early culture in prehistoric China was less visible. However, they carried a steadfast faith as a clan of believers of Yahweh who were religiously distinct and different from all the other people in prehistoric China.

Many children from the line of Cain worshipped pantheons of idols, ghosts, and demons. They practiced shamanism and all kinds of channeling of evil spirits. There were also many atheists among them. Many of them became barbarians foraging food in everywhere they went and always thirst for blood to satisfy their savage way of life. Their population must be consistently numerous as China had been troubled by barbaric invaders throughout her beginning to dynastic history. This constant menace to the rulers of China ultimately led to the erection of the Great Wall of China.

Before the Deluge, the migrated children and descendants from the line of Seth and Cain were the ancestors of the earliest clans and tribes in prehistoric China.

While the migrated children and descendants from the line of Seth and Cain settled and thrived in prehistoric China, their counterpart's daughters in ancient Near East were lust after by fallen angels. Genesis 6:1-3 tells us mankind was genetically corrupted by the grotesque union between fallen angels and earthly women. Their offspring were a race of giants called the Nephilim. The Nephilim committed all kinds of wickedness on earth. They also corrupted other creatures they could lay their hands on. The Nephilim devoured everything even human beings for food. They were like demons from hell terrifying humans and animals for pleasure, food, and blood. The world under the Nephilim was a grotesque and bloody hell on earth. However, the Nephilim were admired by mankind as heroes for their super strength and their divine bloodline from the fallen angels.

The Bible didn't say if the Nephilim had spread to the East or confined to the region in ancient Near East. However, the terrible consequence caused by the Nephilim had left God no choice but to eradicate mankind by a global Deluge. The Deluge killed all mankind including all those sons and daughters of Seth and Cain who had migrated to pre-dynastic China. Only Noah, his three sons: Shem, Ham, and Japheth and their four wives were spared.

After the Deluge, the children and descendants from the line of Shem, Ham, and Japheth repopulated the world. They became the second waves of migrants to wander to distant lands. For those who migrated and settled in China, they became the ancestors of tribes scattered all over pre-dynastic China. Among them was the clan of the descendants from the line of Shem. They were steadfast believers of one God. They were likely the remote ancestor of the Shang people who worshipped Shang-Ti as the supreme God over all gods.

After the Deluge, Noah's three sons expanded human population in ancient Near East. Inevitably, many of them had to search for new lands for food and pastures. Like their predecessors before the

Deluge, many had to depart the biblical homeland to other lands. For those who wandered eastward, they would reach China at the end of the Eurasia continent. This was the normal cause of dispersal of early mankind from the biblical land.

However, two significant biblical events had expedited the movement of people which caused a mass exodus out of the biblical land:

The Curse of Noah (Genesis 9:24-27)

The first event was caused by the offence of Ham inflicted on Noah's nakedness while he was drunk in his tent. No one knew exactly what the offence was; however, it was serious enough for Noah to curse Canaan, the youngest son of Ham that his descendants would become slaves of Shem and Japheth. The curse would trigger a mass exodus of Canaanites and other supportive Hamites out of the biblical land to flee as far away as they could to avoid their descendants to be anyone slaves. China would be one of the distant lands where some of them had fled to where they found safety and freedom from the curse. The children and descendants from the line of Canaan and other supportive Hamites restarted their lives and formed their own tribes in China.

Like Cain's children, Canaan and other Hamites' descendants were astray people. Because of the punishment of the curse by Noah, they were rebellious against God. They practiced all kinds of superstitious rites and worshipped idols for all kinds of carnal and wicked purposes. Frequently, they resorted to violence for solution so they had a very low standard of moral and righteousness. Their way of existence by killing and subduing others made them the dominant people in early China.

Racially, the migrated people from the biblical land to China would be Mongoloid people since they seemed to be the dominant race in the very beginning history of China.

After Ham told Shem and Japheth about Noah's nakedness, both went backward with a garment to cover Noah. For that both were blessed by Noah.⁴

Japheth's descendants were blessed by Noah that they would extend their territory. Racially, Japheth's descendants were mostly of European stocks. And it came to pass that they became daring adventurers and conquerors of new lands in many parts of the world. Their successful expansion and influence outside of their homeland continues into the modern world.

The children of Japheth who had migrated to China were a minority people because Mongoloid people had dominated over pre-dynastic China. Japheth's children were believers of Yahweh but they tended to mix blessing and the will of God with greed and power for self gain. Their westward migration was more successful than their eastward movement. The farthest they expanded in the East was Russia where they ruled and mixed with Asiatic people. Their small number in pre-dynastic China resulted in either they got assimilated into the Mongoloid race by mixed breeding or they got eradicated by the majority Mongoloid race.

Noah blessed Shem's descendants that God would always be with them. This was the most powerful blessing of all than any kind of material blessings. Shem's descendants would be forever guided and watched over by God wherever they went. They would be the messengers and witnesses of God in everywhere they dwell.

The children of Shem who had migrated to China were also a minority people like the Japhethites. Racially, most of them were Middle Eastern brown Caucasians. Their monotheistic faith in Yahweh made them a distinct and godly people with high moral and discipline. They were a unique people being looked up to by other clans and tribes for their values of belief which promoted harmonious and peaceful co-existence.

The Tower Of Babel (11:1-9)

This was the most significant event in the Bible which ultimately divided mankind. Nimrod, the grandson of Ham, was a mighty warrior and feared by people in his time. He was a great king and ruler. His kingdom spread over Babylon, Erech, Akkad and Calneh in ancient Iraq.

The Bible didn't tell us the detail of how Nimrod incited the people of his time to build the tallest tower to reach heaven. However, with mankind speaking in one language, it enabled Nimrod to coerce all people for his lofty project.

The incident of the Tower of Babel confirmed mankind spoke one language since the time of Cain and Abel. Therefore, people who had migrated to China before and after the Deluge till the Towel of Babel incident spoke the universal language of the world. This was significant to know because early clans and tribes established in China before the Tower of Babel had no language barrier. They saw mankind as one species just like they saw animals and wild beasts in their own kind in all color and shapes. In another word they saw Negro, Caucasian, and Mongoloid type of people as simply varieties of human beings in the same species. Thus, they had no discrimination against each other despite of their facial, physical and complexion differences. They accepted each other as one race in one language!

Although God was upset with Nimrod, however, He saw Nimrod was one man's arrogance against Him and not the entire mankind. God was not eager to destroy mankind all over again. God chose to confuse mankind with diversified languages, so Nimrod couldn't unite mankind against Him. God adopted the most ingenious way to destroy Nimrod pride without destroying lives.

The chaos caused by the confusion of languages forced mankind to divide among them. Hundreds if not thousands of groups must have formed by language which they could understand each other. The profound consequence forced each language group to separate from one another to live in separate land. This caused mass exodus of people out of the biblical land to all over the world. And one place where many language groups had fled to was China. Who would know the influx of diversity of people into China after the Tower of Babel had synergized them into a unique people called Chinese and lasted 5,000 years of perpetual history.

The Tower of Babel surely scattered mankind to all corners of the earth.

CHAPTER 2 - ANCIENT MESSENGERS OF YAHWEH TO CHINA

WHO WERE THE ANCIENT MESSENGERS OF YAHWEH IN CHINA? There are only two places in the Book of Genesis where we can find the likely candidates to be the messengers of Yahweh in pre-dynastic China. They were the other sons and daughters begot by the patriarchs in the line of Seth and Shem. Their names were not mentioned in the genealogy from Seth to Noah in Genesis 5:1-32 and in the genealogy from Shem to Abraham in Genesis 10:11-26.

The patriarchs begot many other children over their long life span besides the ones named in the above genealogies. The Book of Genesis didn't say how many other sons and daughters were begot by the patriarchs, however, it must be hundreds if not thousand since they had a very long life.

Many of these other sons and daughters must have departed to distant lands before the Book of Genesis was written. We were told Moses wrote the first five books of the Torah (Genesis, Exodus, Leviticus, Numbers and Deuteronomy). He recorded there were other sons and daughters begot by the patriarchs besides the ones named in the genealogy. Clearly, his intention was to recognize there were also other sons and daughters begot by the patriarchs, but they were not accounted for because either he couldn't trace them or there were too many of them to list in the genealogy. The former difficulty was obvious.

The first genealogy from Adam to Noah in Genesis 5:1-32 mentioned there were other sons and daughters begot by the patriarchs. The last patriarch in the genealogy was Noah. He had only three sons: Shem, Ham, and Japheth and he didn't have any other children. See genealogy 1 below.

GENEALOGY 1 - GENESIS 5:1-32
OTHER SONS & DAUGHTERS OF ADAM TO LAMECH

5:1-5 ... Adam lived 800 years and **had other sons and daughters** ... Adam lived 930 years, and then he died

5:6-8 ... Seth lived 807 years and **had other sons and daughters** ... Seth lived 912 years, and then he died

5:9-11 ... Enosh lived 815 years and **had other sons and daughters** ... Enosh lived 905 years, and then he died

5:12-14 ... Kenan lived 840 years and **had other sons and daughters** ... Kenan lived 910 years, and then he died

5:15-17 ... Mahalalel lived 830 years and **had other sons and daughters** ... Mahalalel lived 895 years, and then he died

5:18-20 ... Jared lived 800 years and **had other sons and daughters** ... Jared lived 962 years, and then he died.

5:21-24 ... Enoch walked with God 300 years and **had other sons and daughters** ... Enoch lived 365 years. Enoch walked with God; then he was no more, because God took him away

5:24-27 ... Methuselah lived 782 years and **had other sons and daughters** ... Methuselah lived 969 years, and then he died

5:28-31 ...Lamech lived 595 years and **had other sons and daughters** ... Lamech lived 777 years, and then he died

5:32 After Noah was 500 years old; he became the father of Shem, Ham and Japheth

The second genealogy from Shem to Abraham in Genesis 11:10-26 also mentioned there were other sons and daughters begot by the patriarchs. The last patriarch in this genealogy line was Terah. Like Noah, he had only three sons. One of them was Abraham. Terah lived 70 years and died. He had the shortest life of all patriarchs. See Genealogy 2 below.

GENEALOGY 2 - GENESIS 11:10-26
OTHER SONS & DAUGHTERS OF SHEM TO TERAH

11:10-11 … Shem lived 500 years and **had other sons and daughters**

11:12-13 … Arphaxad lived 403 years and **had other sons and daughters**

11:14-15 … Shelah lived 403 years and **had other sons and daughters**

11:16-17 … Eber lived 430 years and **had other sons and daughters**

11:18-19 … Peleg lived 209 years and **had other sons and daughters**

11:20-21 … Reu lived 207 years and **had other sons and daughters**

11:22-23 … Serug lived 200 years and **had other sons and daughters**

11:24-25 … Nahor lived 119 years and **had other sons and daughters**

11:26 After Terah had lived 70 years; he became the father of Abram, Nahor, and Haran

The Book of Genesis had no information about where the other sons and daughters in the above two genealogies went and what happened to them. We could only imagine they had departed to distant land and forever forgotten by their families.

Early humans migrated from Eden to all over the world since the dawn of mankind. The Bible didn't tell us where early humans migrated to. To those early humans who ventured afar, they would lose contact and eventually forgotten by their families back home. If they survived their journey and settled in their chosen new land, their posterity would slowly but surely transformed into aboriginal people and developed their own unique culture. Over time their posterity assumed they were originated from the land where they dwelled and totally forgot where their remote ancestors came from.

This was what happened to many races after their remote ancestors journeyed afar from the biblical homeland to their new land. Their ancestors started a new beginning in the new land. After a long period of time their posterity gradually forgot their biblical origin. All they could remember was vague and distorted stories passed down to them generation after generation until those stories became myths and legends.

After Adam and Eve were expelled to the East of Eden (in ancient Iraq), their first two sons were Cain and Abel. Cain murdered Abel out of jealousy for being favored by God. God replaced Abel with Seth to be His planned seed for the line of the future coming of the Messiah.

The Bible didn't give an account of Seth's character and what sort of man he was. We can only learn about Seth from Josephus, the Jewish

Historian, in his book *Antiquities of the Jews*. Josephus wrote that Seth was a virtuous and righteous man that his descendants imitated his character for seven generations! His descendants all lived in harmony for seven generations until they gone astray in the time of Noah. From Josephus, we could picture what kind of sons and daughters from the line of Seth were. They were a people of love, virtue, righteousness, and kindness.

Seth's line of other children in Genesis 5:1-32 were the first wave of migrants to venture to distant lands including China. Unfortunately, mankind was corrupted by fallen angels; in the end all living things were killed by the Deluge sent down by God. Thus, traces of the other sons and daughters from the line of Seth that had migrated to distant lands became more obscure. Worst of all, evidences of their existence in other lands including China had all been totally wiped out by the Deluge.

After the Deluge, the line of Shem succeeded the line of Seth to be the blessed line for the coming of the Messiah. They were the second wave of Yahweh messengers to migrate to distant lands including China.

Shem was also a virtuous and righteous man worthy of God's blessing to carry the sacred line. Among Noah's three sons, the children from the line of Shem were the most faithful to Yahweh. They practiced their faith vehemently under the guidance of their righteous and obedient patriarch of Yahweh. They were a people of love, virtue and righteousness like the children of Seth.

We learnt from the Bible that Ham offended his naked father, Noah, while he was drunk inside his tent. No one knew exactly what the offence was but it must have caused a great deal of shame and disgrace to Noah.

Shem and Japheth went backward inside the tent with a garment to cover their drunken and naked father. From this instance we could picture Shem and Japheth possessed good moral character and had total respect for their father.

The departed other sons and daughters of Shem remembered the stories happened in the Biblical homeland. From the seven-day Genesis of the world, the creation of Adam and Eve to the Deluge that God sent down to destroy mankind; they passed down their memory to their descendant generation after generation. Thus, they were truly the messengers and storytellers of Yahweh in everywhere they wandered and dwelled.

We have no idea of how many other sons and daughters in Genesis 5:1-32 and in Genesis 10:11-26 had departed to other lands. Some of them might have moved to places within contactable distance with their patriarch and family. Because many of their names were not mentioned in the genealogy list, we have to assume they must have gone far away and the author of the Book of Genesis couldn't trace them from their descendants.

Surely, the departed other sons and daughters of Seth and Shem faced many unknown challenges in their eastward journey. Their adventure would resemble modern astronauts in a spaceship flying out of the Solar System without knowing what challenges they would face in the galaxies or planets where they are heading. In both cases, the other sons and daughters and the astronauts would be assumed dead if they didn't return to tell their adventure. Surely, very few had returned home after they traveled farther and farther away from their Biblical homeland. Finally, they were forgotten by their families and friends back home. They were like those astronauts in the spaceship traveling many light years afar to a distant planet where their families on Earth had ceased to remember them.

These forgotten other sons and daughters of Shem were the suspects of this book who had wandered to early China. They and their descendants were the ones who seeded the knowledge of God in the legendary beginning of China.

Unfortunately, the Book of Genesis didn't record any Table of Nations found by the line of Seth and the line of Cain (their descendants also all killed by the Deluge). Thus, we had no way of knowing what clans, tribes, or nations were found by the children of Seth and Cain in the antediluvian world.

Chapter 10 of the Book of Genesis listed the Table of Nations found by the line of Shem, Ham, and Japheth in the postdiluvian world. However, it couldn't be a complete list of all the nations in the world because no one knew if there were tribes and nations found beyond the contactable region outside ancient Near East by descendant of the other sons and daughters who had departed to distant land.

In early China, shadow of the other sons and daughters and their descendants from the line of Shem appeared as the Shang people who worshipped a supreme god called Shang-Ti. How did the Shang people adopt monotheism? How could the Shang people invent monotheism when early people in China indulged in the practice of shamanism, animism, and worship of ancestors, idols, ghosts, sun, moon, and mountain?

How strange for one clan in early China to embrace monotheism alone in a world of diverse superstitions. The forefather of the Shang people must believe a religion of one supreme-god. Who else could be the remote ancestors of the Shang people? Could they be the other sons and daughters of Shem who believed in a supreme god and had migrated to China?

The Shang people were definitely a religious people. Tang, the founder of the Shang people, was a devoted patriarch of Shang-Ti. He openly declared to his people that he feared Shang-Ti very much and wouldn't disobey His will.² Tang confession paralleled the inexorable obedience of the patriarchs in the line of Shem. Was this pure coincidence or evidence of Tang's patriarch faith inherited from his ancestors from the line of Shem? After Tang overthrown the last Xia emperor, Tang became the first emperor of the Shang Dynasty. Shang-Ti became the state God of China.

Although no solid evidence can substantiate the claim that the Shang people were the descendant from the line of Shem, however, undisputed evidences of the Shang people believed in a supreme deity, a kingdom in heaven, and the mandate of heaven (will of God) were strong indications that the believers of Yahweh had set foot in China. For how did the Shang people acquire such knowledge if steadfast believers of Yahweh hadn't brought their faith to China?

The other sons and daughters of Seth and Shem in Genesis 5:1-32 and Genesis 10:11-26 were the forgotten people in the Bible. Some of them had reached pre-dynastic China. They were the ones who seeded the knowledge of the God of the Bible in the beginning of China. Their loving and righteous character had profoundly impacted early Chinese people to practice love, virtue and righteousness. They were the unsung heroes of teachers of love and righteousness. Their descendant arose as the Shang people who worshipped Yahweh by the name of Shang-Ti. They were one of the significant ancestors of the Chinese people.

CHAPTER 3 – THE EAST

The EAST IN THE BIBLE was a forsaken place where people traveled there would vanish into oblivion. The other sons and daughters of Seth and Shem who migrated to China were forever forgotten by their family back home. Their names didn't make it in the genealogy in Genesis 5:1-32 and Genesis 11:10-26.

East Asia is an obscure place in the Bible. Ancient people in the biblical land had very little knowledge of what lies beyond Central Asia. Ancient nomads who departed ancient Near East and Central Asia to the East would be gone forever. It would be a long and difficult journey which required arduous negotiation through many rough terrains and precarious climate while turning back was equally dangerous.

The authors of the Bible had no knowledge of the enormity and geography of East Asia. God didn't disclose to all the authors of the 66 books of the Bible any information about East Asia. For whatever purpose, God chose to keep the East away from His prophets and preachers. Even Apostle Paul was warned not to travel to the East to preach God's words.[1] The East was a perverted place where God allowed the Devil to exert maximum influence over humans.

Cain and Abel were the first two humans born outside in the east of Eden. It was no surprise that Cain was the first human to commit murder against his brother in the corrupted East. Even the East wind was a destructive force which God and his prophets would call upon to destroy sinners.

For whatever reason, people in the East tend to be aggressive, belligerent, violent, intolerant, unforgiving, and less merciful by character despite their glorious ancient civilization had produced profound philosophies, diverse religions of love, earliest scientific knowledge, inventions, and mankind first writing system.

In modern China, human right and democracy are constant issues criticized by the United Nations. China ruthless murdered of her young students with tanks and machine guns in Tiananmen Square Massacre on June 4, 1989 shocked the world. In recent years, the persecution of the followers of Falun Gong disgusted the world why China is so hysterical to see such practitioners of spiritual and healing exercise as a condemned threat to her national security.

In North Korea, President Kim Jong-il cares more about military build up and develop nuclear bomb than to feed her starving people. North and South Koreans continue to see each other as a potential invader in their divided territory. The declaration of war between the two sides can be trigger by any trivial thing that can be used as an excuse to destroy the other side.

In the Indian subcontinent, Hindus and Sikhs are always ready to kill each other for religious differences. Between the border of Pakistan and India, armies from both sides glare at each other with gnawing teeth and ready to open fire at any second. Even scarier is their nuclear missiles in secret places are only a finger tip away from firing towards each other land for the big kill.

In the Middle East, Arabs, Palestinians, and Muslim extremes continue their never ending hostility towards Israel. For whatever reason, the feud between the Jews and the Palestinians became an eternal mission for their descendants to hate and kill each other despite they came from the same ancestry of Abraham.

God was very specific where He wanted Adam and Eve to restart their life after they committed the original sin. God expelled them to the east of Eden. Children born outside of Eden carried the original sin to the East before any other place in the world. God seemed to have a cleansing purpose for the East where sufferings are harsher and longer to remind mankind of the original sin. Could this be why people in the East tend to have a mindset of enmity, selfishness, greed, hate, and revenge with very little interest in peaceful coexistence with other races?

On the other hand, the impact of Christianity in the West had induced westerners to embrace a gentler and peaceful mindset. The teachings of Jesus Christ's love thy neighbor as thy self and forgiveness have tamed westerners to be a more open minded and tolerant people than Easterners.

Ancient Chinese had no idea of how far the West was exactly like the authors of the Bible who had no idea of how far the East was. The strangest thing was people in the West never thought of the East as a place of utopia while ancient people in the East saw the West was the ultimate utopia.

Could this mysterious notion of the West the remnant memory of the Garden of Eden? If it were, such idea must be brought to early China by people who were believers of Yahweh. Could this people come from the line of Shem?

Add 1 Concluding Paragraph

CHAPTER 4 - THE FIRST CHINESE PEOPLE

TO TRACE THE FIRST PEOPLE appeared in the beginning time of China is like finding a needle in the bottom of the sea. Paleolithic and Neolithic sites were found in many places all over China. Some sites are dated earlier than others but the racial type of the people who left behind their traces of existence couldn't be firmly identified. Perhaps we shouldn't expect only one homogenous people occupied in the beginning time of China. To say there was just one homogeneous people existed in early China would be naive and would limit our understanding in the origin of Chinese people.

Up to the time of this writing there is no concrete archaeological evidence to substantiate the existence of the Xia dynasty (2205-1766 BC), the first dynasty of China. The Xia dynasty was likely a tribal dynasty that lived in tents and simple settlement. The Xia people had no Chinese writing system, thus, no records of any kind were passed down. Many of their legends and stories were passed down by mouth and later recorded in the Book of History. Xia dynasty remains to be an important part of Chinese history that Chinese historians can't afford to refute it as fiction.

So far archaeologists have only discovered sites and palaces associated with the Shang dynasty (1766-1122 BC) but not the Xia. The Shang dynasty lasted 644 years before it was overthrown and replaced by the Zhou dynasty (1122-255 BC).

The people of Xia, Shang, and Zhou dynasty could be a heterogeneous people where the Mongoloids were the majority while the Caucasians and Negroes were the minority. The diversity of people in the beginning of China was why early Chinese people called their world "Middle Kingdom", the centre of the world where all races from the four corners of the earth converged. The diversity of people in early China seeded the intellectual ingredients for the rise of Chinese civilization.

Emperor Shih Huang Ti ("The First Emperor") was the first dynastic emperor to unite China in 221 BC. He was a brilliant conqueror but a tyrant. However, his tyranny helped to solidify his diversified subjects. He imposed a uniform writing of Chinese characters on all his subjects throughout China. Thereafter, Chinese characters became a powerful gel in the cultural unification of China for over 2,200 years. Emperor Shih-Huang-Ti united his subjects into one giant cultural race by Chinese writing.

By the time of Shih Huang Ti (The First Emperor), the Mongoloid people had established themselves as the dominant people in China. The discovery of the tomb of Emperor Shih Huang Ti where thousands of lively and life-size Terra Cotta soldiers lined up in battle formation testified the

Mongoloid people had become the master race in ancient China. By this time the remaining Caucasians and Negroes who were still in China had become an invisible minority.

Sadly, the poverty of ancient Chinese records hampered the study of origin of the Chinese people. The Book of History (Shu Ching) was the oldest books in China. It was written before the Qin dynasty. It shed light on events and kingship in the early legendary dynasties but it was not a history book. It was a book of announcements and letters from the tribal emperors and officials during the Xia, Shang, and Zhou dynasties.

Confucius had used this book as reference to teach his students. Chinese Historians suspect Confucius edited the Book of History but it is impossible to prove. Confucius should obtain plenty of knowledge about the past since he had access to many antique books before his time. However, being the most revered scholar in his time he seemed reluctant to elaborate what he knew about the past. Even in his teaching, Confucius made little references to the type of races appeared in prehistory and languages. He answered briefly when only asked by his students in this topic.

We have no way of knowing if Confucius and other scholars in his time knew if the legendary sages, Yellow Emperor, and early benevolent emperors were fictional or not and if they were

Mongoloid or not. But one thing for sure, Confucius didn't refute any legends nor discarded them as myths. It seemed he was withholding some unverifiable truth that could be controversial or damaging his name. If there was one person who was more than qualified to clarify the legendary history of China, it would be Confucius. But he didn't clarify it for history sake or for the Chinese race's sake.

In modern China, the Han people represent more than 93% of the population.³ The Han people are regarded as the pure Chinese people. The rest is composed of 55 minorities including non-Chinese people such as Koreans, Mongolians, Asiatic Turks, Uyghurs, Tartars, Russians, Tibetans, and other minorities.

Many ethnic groups in China don't regard themselves as Chinese by race but they accept their Chinese nationality. These non-Chinese people were historical orphans of their ancestors who came to China in ancient time and had been absorbed by the Chinese as a minority people.

The territory of China stretches from north to south through 49 degree latitude in the most eastern part of the Eurasia continent. The size of China is almost 10 millions sq km. Two rivers divided this huge land and marked her north and south territories by the Yellow River in the north and the Yangtze River in the south. The eastern edge of China is a long coastline facing the Pacific Ocean. China was the last territory where ancient nomads ended their journey in the East.

Ancient nomads traveled from the land of the Bible had to pass through Central Asia to go to the East. They had to negotiate a long journey of ruthless terrains, mountainous ranges, arid steppes, and scorching deserts to reach the western border of China. Once they entered China they would be isolated from the rest of the world because leaving China posed equal insurmountable challenges as the way in.

Another route to China would be along the coastline via Saudi Arabia to India, Southeast Asia then to southern China. This route had fewer obstacles to overcome and under warmer climate. This was the route taken by primitive Africans from Africa to Australia and New Zealand around 60,000-50,000 years ago.

Northern China was mostly a ghost land before the Ice Sheet retreated around 12,000 years ago. There were small pockets of ancient nomads scattered in the frigid land of China during the last Ice age. No one knew when humans arrived in Siberia. The Paleo-Siberians were the first people to appear in Siberia. They were mostly Mongoloids although some historians might see the Native American as a separate race from the Mongoloid. To me, they were the remote ancestral stock of the Mongoloid people in East Asia.

Around 18,000 years ago, Paleo-Siberians who reached the northeastern edge of Siberia crossed the frozen Bering Strait to Alaska.[5] Those who settled in the new promised land of North America evolved into different tribes of American Indians. One school of archaeological theory believes that there were three separate waves of migration to America from the Siberian mainland over thousands years of time. Thus, there could be other people especially the Caucasians who might accompany the Mongoloid people in the later waves of migration.

Not all Paleo-Siberians who reached the northeastern tip of Siberia crossed to the other side of the frozen Bering Strait. Some had stayed behind. Some retreated southward all the way to northeastern China, Mongolia, the Korea peninsula, and Japan. This was how Mongoloid people scattered all over Northeast Asia.

Japan is the place where the earliest ceramic potteries dated 10,000 years ago were found.[6] Who else could have reached Japan at such early time other than the Paleo-Siberians who were Mongoloid people? They made it to northern Japan by either crossed the frozen Japan Sea to Siberia around 30,000 years ago or by floating on primitive raft after the Ice retreated

The people I am talking here were Homo *italic* sapiens. They possessed physical attributes like modern humans. I am not talking about ape men or other hominoids classified as ancestors of man by evolutionists. Therefore, don't be confused why this book doesn't mention the *Peking Man* (dated 500,000 years ago) as the earliest ancestor of Chinese people. *Peking Man* is not a Homo sapiens. God didn't create Peking Man to be the first man of mankind. Peking Man is a creature not man. Adam is the first man that God created to be the father of the human race. So don't confused Paleo-Siberians were evolved from *Peking Man*.

Paleo Siberians were Mongoloid type of people although they could be accompanied by Caucasian and Negro type of people in their migration to Siberia. We had no way of knowing if the Paleo Siberians were 100% homogeneous people. However, their descendants are visibly Mongoloids such as the Mongolians, Koreans, Japanese, northern Chinese, Eskimos, and the Native American Indians.

Prehistoric China was a huge land open to ancient nomads coming from all over the world. How could we assume only Mongoloid people occupied China right from the beginning of time? Chinese history recorded there were diversified tribes appeared in early China. Were they all Mongoloid people?

Since the dawn of prehistory, there was no solid evidence in who was the first type of people inhabited China. Mongoloid people was generally seen as the beginning race at the dawn of Chinese history, however, Caucasian and Negro nomads had also entered prehistoric China. Who could be sure Caucasians and Negroes weren't part of the early population in China?

The late Chinese archaeologist, Li Chi, after compared the skulls of Shang people with other Neolithic skulls unearthed in archaeological sites in China detected a range of variation of cephalic indexes of skulls to be non-homogeneity. He hinted such variations were due to an infusion of a broader headed element accompanied the establishment of the imperial power of Shang in North China (see "Shang Civilization" by Kwang Chih Chang P.331-332). Who were the broader headed elements?

I believed Li was referring to Caucasian people who generally had a broader head and neck.

In another study of human skulls from the Shang sites in An Yang by another Chinese archaeologist, Yang Hsi Mei; he found different types of humans inhabited in Shang China. Yang subdivided the morphological structure of the skulls he studied into five subgroups (see "Shang Civilization" by Kwang Chih Chang P.332-334):

Subgroup I - The Classical Mongoloid type
Subgroup II - The Oceanic Negroid type
Subgroup III - The Caucasoid type
Subgroup IV - The Eskimo type
Subgroup V - An unnamed type

Yang found the number of Mongoloid type of skulls outnumbered all the other subgroups. Clearly, the Mongoloids were the dominant race but the discovery of Caucasian and Negro type of skulls revealed there were three morphological types of humans coexisted in early China. The skulls from the Shang site in An-Yang confirmed the diversity of races in early China.

Furthermore, if there were only one homogenous people, we would find a pattern of uniform tradition, custom, and way of life spread across early China because such habits of life would pass from generation to generation and from place to place with little changes. This was not the case in early China.

Early China exhibited diverse cultural development which indicated the diversity of people inhabited the land. There were distinct cultural development arose separately in different places in China around 5000 to 3000 BC. Most notably, the Yangshao culture; Dawenkou culture; Hemudu culture; Majiabang culture; Mayjiayao culture; Banshan culture; Machang culture and; Longshan culture. These separate cultural developments came from different people who pursued different life style in crop planting, farming, fishing, and collective dwelling. Their distinct culture suggested they came from different origins and they might not be Mongoloid people.

Diverse cultures in early China dictated the way of life of early Chinese people. The early settlers in north and south China even ate differently. Rice, the main diet of southern Chinese, began cultivation in the south while northern Chinese cultivated the millet which became the main diet in the north. But the cradle of Chinese civilization arose along the Yellow River in the north. This could be the result of outside influence was stronger in the north than in the south. Particular the spreading of knowledge and idea from ancient Near East would impact the early people in northern China quicker than the south.

Early ancient Chinese records mentioned there were foreign tribes in the beginning history of China. The well known tribes were the Yi in the northeast; the Man in the south; the Rong in the West and; the Di in the north. These four tribes were fearsome people always ready to make trouble with the tribes in China. They were barbarians of the East. Chinese historians tend to assume they were all Mongoloid type of people. But were they?

The appearance of foreign invaders in early China confirmed that the Mongoloid Chinese were not the only people occupied the vast land of China. Therefore, we must not rule out other races had also set foot on China soil and had coexisted with the Mongoloid Chinese in the beginning time of China.

Some of the tribes wandered into early China could be Europeans. Chinese archaeologists have dug up mummies with European facial features in Taklamakan Desert of Tarim Basim in the western edge of China.¹⁰ Many mummies are currently displayed in the museums of Ürümchi, the capital of the Uyghur Autonomous Region. Some of these mummies were dated to 4,000 years old.

Ancient European nomads probably entered China in small groups, thus, they were an invisible minority in the Mongoloid population. Historians are shock by their discovery for they would never imagine ancient European nomads had wandered so far and so deep into China at such remote time.

To the west of China is Russia. There were Europeans and Mongoloids coexisting in Russia since the 2nd millennium BC (4,000 years ago). The white Russians are of European stocks. Who could discard the possibility that Russian nomads had wandered into China and even mixed with the Mongoloids long before Yellow Emperor appeared?

The discovery of European mummies in Tarim Basin was evidences of diverse races of nomads had wandered into China more than anyone imagine.

Chinese historians can no longer rule out the possibility that ancient Europeans had penetrated China 4,000 years ago and might have mixed with the Mongoloid Chinese.

Equally, who could discard the possibility that the Negroes had entered and settled in Paleolithic China? The earliest Negroes migrated out of Africa 60,000 years ago. They wandered afar to Australia and New Zealand in a southerly route from Africa and established colonies along the way through India, and Southeast Asia. Some of their descendants might have entered southern China and some might have wandered to northern China as well. The African Negroes could be the first people to step foot in southern China. Their ancestors had migrated out of Africa to the East long before any other races. They might be the first settlers in southern China until the Mongoloid race arrived and displaced them outside of China.

Although my notion might be far fetched to some readers, however, the homogeneity of one race in a land didn't happen perfectly right from the beginning of time. Rather, history tells us that diversity and the consequence of interaction and competition between races in a land resulted in the domination and homogeneity of one race and the displacement of other races to other lands.

The Mongoloid race might not be the first people to occupy China. The only thing we can be sure of is that the Mongoloids were dominant people in the beginning of China. They had coexisted with other minority races and gradually blended with them producing a wide variety of beautiful Chinese faces. A multi-racial beginning of early China was the catalyst to the rise of Chinese civilization.

Sculpted Images of Negro, Caucasian, and Mongoloid faces could be seen on Neolithic potteries, relics, and statues unearthed from various archaeological sites in China. Readers can find photos of these images on archaeological objects in archaeology books available in local libraries and on the Internet. Because of the difficulty in obtaining print permission of these photos for this book, I would be happy to email you a list of names of books where these photos could be found. Please email to kenkwok@telus.net with the subject line "Request for Chinese Relics Listing". I will respond back to you within 48 hours or as soon as I can.

To Chinese Christians who yearn for the truth of our biblical heritage, our heart is echoed by the poem "Prayer" written by Wen Yiduo, a remarkable cultural figure of post-imperial China's in the early twentieth century.

PRAYER by Wen Yiduo, 1927 [12]

Please tell me, who are the Chinese?
Show me how to cherish memory.
Please tell me of this people's greatness
Softly tell me; don't shout it out.

Please tell me, who are the Chinese?
In whose hearts are the hearts of Yao and Shun;
Whose blood is the blood of Jing Ke and Nie Zheng?
Who are the children of Shennong and Huangdi?

You tell me that wisdom came so strangely,
You say it was a present brought by the river horse,
You even tell me that this song's rhythm
Was first handed down by the nine-hued phoenix.

Who will tell of the Gobi's silence?
And the five peaks' majesty? And tell me too
That Mount Tai's stone drops still drip patiently,
And that the Yangtze and Yellow rivers still flow calmly?
Tell me again, which drop of pure tear
Is the grief Confucius cried for the dead unicorn?
Which fool will tell me truly?
Of the laughing of Zhuang Zhou, Chunyu Kun, and Dongfang Shuo?

Please tell me, who are the Chinese?
Show me how to cherish memory.
Please tell me of this people's greatness.
Softly tell me; don't shout it out.

CHAPTER 5 – SON OF HEAVEN

WHY DID ANCIENT KING, ruler, and emperor in many cultures were called the "Son of God" or the "Son of Heaven"? How did they come up with such title? Could the title "Son of Heaven" derived from actual event in the remote past where mighty men and renowned men of old as described in the Bible were born of gods?

All ancient civilizations had myths about godly humans who ruled their world. Many cultures in the ancient world all converged to a single concept that their king, ruler or emperor was a divine descendant who carried the bloodline of their god. Why did so many ancient cultures vehemently embrace the concept of their earthly king, ruler or emperor was of heaven or god? Could there be some truth to such concept was derived from actual union between earthly women and godly beings from out of this world?

In ancient China, Chinese emperor was also called the "Son of Heaven". In later dynasties, the title was replaced by the "Son of Dragon". From then on Chinese people called themselves the descendants of the Dragon. Without any deliberate collaboration, this divine title was adopted universally by people in the ancient world to raise their ruler to a godly status. Why? The answer is found in the Book of Genesis of the Bible.

Genesis 6:1-4 recorded there were interbreeding between daughters of men and fallen angels whom the Bible called the Sons of God. They took the daughters of men anyone they chose as wives. The offspring of the Sons of God were called Nephilim. They were giants of great statute and great strength. The Nephilim were a violent and wicked race. They even corrupted other creatures they could lay their hands on. And they devoured everything including humans for food and blood.

Despite of the Nephilim violence and perversion, mankind adored them as heroes and mighty men and worshipped them as great leaders. God grieved that mankind was corrupted by the unholy breeding of humans and angelic beings. In order to eradicate the Nephilim and the corrupted mankind, God had to destroy them all by a global Deluge. God spared Noah, his three sons and their wives for rebuilding mankind after the Deluge.

However, several generations later after the Deluge, descendants of the Nephilim reappeared on the face of the Earth! In the Book of Number verse 13:33, the scouts sent by Moses and Aaron returned and reported that they saw the descendants of Anak who were descendants from the Nephilim. The scouts reported they looked like grasshoppers to the Anak giants. Undoubtedly, what they saw were giants. Goliath, the Palestinian giant, killed by King David was another example of the descendants of

Nephilim reappeared as human population expanded after the Deluge.

How did the Nephilim resurge from their supposedly total demise in the Deluge? Did another group of fallen angels come down to corrupt the daughters of men? Did the wives of Shem, Ham, and Japheth carry suppressed DNA genes of the Nephilim passed down to them by their parents who were part of mankind infected by the interbreeding? The latter possibility is likely.

Earthly men had no chance to compete with the Nephilim as their number increased on earth. They were the mutated X-men in the ancient world. They were huge giant who could tear any man into pieces and devour them for food. They were undoubtedly mighty men whom earthly people looked up to for their super strength and great stature.

Surely, any race, tribe, and nation would want a godly and mighty ruler to protect them. The idea of honoring king, ruler, and emperor as son of heaven was born in the time where the Nephilim ruled the earth. Despite the Nephilim wickedness, earthly men revered them as super heroes and demigods. From then onward, mankind wanted their king, ruler, or emperor to be the son of heaven who possessed the bloodline of their god or gods. This concept must have passed down generation after generation in many races from their remote ancestors in the biblical land. They preserved the concept of the divine king, ruler or emperor from the story of the mighty Nephilim.

Who were the Sons of God in the Bible? There are two interpretations cf Sons of God by biblical scholars:

FIRST INTERPRETATION

The first interpretation sees the sons of God as angels. The name "Sons of God" was mentioned a few times in the Bible:

- Job 38:4-7 "...when the morning stars sang together and all the *Sons of God* shouted for joy"

- Job 1:6 "Now there was a day when the *Sons of God* came to present themselves before the Lord ..."

- Daniel 3:24-25 "Then King Nebuchadnezzar leaped to his feet in amazement ... I see four men walking around in the fire ... and the fourth looks like a *son of the gods*..."

- Daniel 3:28 "Then Nebuchadnezzar said, "Praise be to the God of Shadrach, Meshach and Abednego who sent his *angel* and rescued his servants ..."

In the New International Version, the name "Son of God" is replaced by "Angel". The sons of God are seen as angelic beings. God created the angels before He created man. The Bible tells us angels are exceptional beautiful spiritual beings.

Lucifer, the chief archangel of God, was the most beautiful angel in heaven created by God. Unfortunately, his pride blinded him to believe that he could replace God. Lucifer rebelled against God with one third of the angels in heaven. But he was crushed and cast down to earth with his defeated angels.

The first interpretation of the Sons of God is credible because the offspring of the unholy union between female humans and angels produced giants. Obviously, the Nephilim giants were the result of crossbred between two separate species with incomparable but manipulative biological genes. However, this explanation raises one apparent question: Do angels have physical attributes that could enable them to breed with earthly women?

Angels are spiritual beings and earthly humans are flesh and blood beings. Earthly humans can't transform into a spiritual being by his or her physical power. It is impossible. However, angels are spiritual beings and can transform themselves into another form of being. This is no imagination. The Bible clearly recorded in many occasions that angels appeared in human form. If angels were simply an invisible form of energy and unchangeable, those humanly angels saw by people in the Bible must be something else. I believe angels have certain level of power to transform themselves into physical form where they can interact with mankind.

SECOND INTERPRETATION

The second interpretation sees the Sons of God as earthly men from the line of Seth.² Because of Seth's virtuous character, his descendants were regarded as the pure and righteous stock of mankind as opposed to the descendants from the line of Cain who were a perverted and wicked people. Seth's line was not allowed to mix with the line of Cain. Unfortunately, as it always happened, the males from the line of Seth were overcome by the beauty of the daughters of the line of Cain. They were willing to forfeit their sacred purity in exchange for beautiful women from the line of Cain as wives.

The second interpretation is miserably weak. First of all, why did the sons of Seth have to find wives from the daughters of Cain? Couldn't they find women from their own people?

Secondly, were the women in Seth's line uglier than the daughters from the line of Cain? Why did the males from the line of Seth have to lust after the women from the line of Cain and not lust after the women of their own kind? Were the women from the line of Seth un-sexy and unattractive?

Thirdly, if both Seth and Cain's descendants were ordinary human beings, why did their offspring was born giants? Who caused the genetic abnormality in their offspring? The Nephilim giants were irrefutable evidence that the interbreeding was between two separate kinds of beings. If they were all human beings, the abnormality of their offspring wouldn't happen.

The second interpretation was a weak theory and undermined the power of angels who couldn't interact with earthly people.

Jesus is a resounding testimony that spiritual beings and earthly women could produce offspring. Jesus was the Son of God through His divine intervention with Virgin Mary. Jesus is a flesh and blood human being as a result of God and Virgin Mary sacred union. We seldom question how God and Virgin Mary could produce a baby without physical intercourse? God didn't create Jesus. God begot Jesus in a divine union with a flesh and blood earthly woman who born Him a flesh and blood son.

We question if angels could breed with humans or not, but we didn't question how God could produce a son with a virgin. If God, a divine spiritual being, could inseminate Virgin Mary to give birth to a baby, then why can't we accept angels could have certain level of power to interbreed with earthly women?

The birth of Jesus reminds us that God, angels, and man are in very close relationship. God said "let us made man in our images and in our likeness." Man and angels were made in the images of God. Therefore, man also possesses the spiritual attributes of God and the angels. The image of God is the common denominator connecting God, angels and man. Man can have intimate relationship with God and angels in many sacred ways. Unfortunately, those fallen angels who lusted after earthly women chose to abuse their angelic power instead of using it to protect mankind.

Angels are created by God for the spiritual realm. They are spiritual beings and possess the power to manifest in human form. In many ancient cultures, angels are depicted in human body with a pair of feathery wings on the back. However, angels were never depicted to have wings in both Old and New Testament. Rather they were depicted like a human being with no fancy wings.

The strangest thing about the encounter of angels in the stories of the Bible was that angel(s) could be easily recognized by the person who saw them. In Genesis chapter 18 and 19, when Abraham saw three strangers approached his tent, he immediately bowed to them. How could Abraham recognize they were angels? Abraham didn't see any wings on the back of the three strangers who looked 100% human being! Not only that, the three angels later ate the bread prepared for them and let Abraham washed their human feet with water. Were the three strangers a human or were they an angel? To further confuse the identity of the three strangers, they all transformed into God Himself before they departed for Sodom and Gomorrah.

Abraham must have seen something right away that distinguished the three strangers to be angels. Did Abraham see distinguishable color of hairs, eyeballs, and complexion on the three strangers that were different from earthly people? Abraham and his people were typical Middle Eastern people who were either Negroes or Caucasians with dark hairs, eyeballs, and brown to dark complexion. If the three strangers who approached Abraham's tent had blonde, brunette or red hairs; blue or green eyeballs and; white complexion, it would make them look different from the people in Abraham world. The appearance of three European Caucasians enabled Abraham to recognize them they were angels.

Furthermore, the three strangers left Abraham and went to Sodom and Gomorrah that evening. As soon as the entered the city, they were immediately identified as angels by a crowd of perverted people who approached them for sexual pleasure. Again, the color of their hairs, eyeballs, and complexion were noticeable different from the Negroes and brown Caucasian people in Abraham world.

The appearance of angels in the form of European Caucasian is not a racist idea to promote the superiority of white people. In the Book of Enoch(a book supposedly written by Enoch but was not included in the collections of the Bible) mentioned Lamech, the father of Noah, was terrified to see baby Noah was born with flesh as white as snow, woolly white hairs, and color eyeballs that glowed and shone like the sun.³ The latter phenomenon could be the color and transparent eyeballs which glowed like a reflective mirror against the candles in a dimly lit room at night. The shone like the sun part must be literal exaggeration to emphasize the effect of the color eyeballs in the dark.

The story of the birth of Noah seemed to suggest that people born with white complexion, color eyeballs and hairs had something to do with the interbreeding between human and angel. Obviously, this was why Lamech suspected baby Noah was born a child of angel because of his apparent European features. In Noah world, light brown to dark people were the common earthly people, therefore, European Caucasians were seen as a new breed of humans derived from the offspring of angels with the daughters of men.

Scientifically, we are told that early humans who migrated to the cold region on earth (mainly in northern hemisphere in Europe) had changed physically due to the rigid cold climate and the lack of sufficient sunlight in their living environment.⁴ These physical changes turned their skin white, eyeballs and hairs colored, and nose taller, narrower, and longer to warm the cold air they breathed in. Their posterity became the Europeans.

However, the remaining descendants of the Paleo-Siberians who live in the harshest and coldest climate in northern Siberia such as the Nenets, Nganasans, Sel'Kups, Khants, Mansis, and Dolgans, and Eskimos retained their Asiatic genetic traits after 18,000 years of existence in Siberia. Their yellowish skin hadn't turned white, and their eyeballs and hairs remain brown to dark.

The difference of effect in cold region on earth between those who evolved into Europeans and those remained Asiatic could be due to the type of diet they ate. One school of scientific thinking believes the latter consumed a lot of vitamin A and D from fishes and whales which were the principal food in the region where they hunted and lived. This helped to reduce the physical changes required for adaptation to their environment.

I am not a scientist or biologist; therefore, I can't speak affirmatively how humans mutated into different type of races. However, it was clear that Lamech was shock to see Noah was born with woolly white hairs, color eyeballs, and skin as white as snow. The cause of such fear suggested that Lamech identified what earthly people should look like and what mixed people by angels and humans look like. The latter was distinguished by the white complexion, colorful eyeballs and hairs of the European.

In ancient China, barbarians that raid Chinese borders were called "Foreign Devil". In strict Chinese translation, the name "Foreign Devil" meant foreign ghost. The foreign part referred to the origin of place came from outside of China. The ghost part described the barbarians who raid Chinese land resembled the dead people in paled and bloodless skin.

Ghost is a spirit of dead people. Ancient Chinese saw white people as evil ghosts because of their white complexion and their mischievous raid into Chinese land. The fact that ancient Chinese saw fair skinned barbarians as ghost echoed the fear of Lamech who saw baby Noah born with white skin, color eyeballs and hairs. Both ancient Chinese and Lamech saw European Caucasians were some kind of extraterrestrial beings different from the earthly people who had darker complexion and mono-color features.

Angels are beautiful and majestic spiritual beings created by God. Before Lucifer rebelled against God, he was created the second most beautiful spiritual being after God.⁵ Imagine how beautiful and glamorous the rest of the angels must be. I believe angels can transmit their colorful angelic attributes to human beings through human eyes, hairs, and skin.

European Caucasians were born with whiter skin and colorful features than any other races. They are a unique race born with symmetrical facial features and bright colorful eyeballs and hairs. I wonder if they had inherited some angelic attributes passed down to them from the sons of God who took daughters of men as wives in Genesis 6:1-4.

In ancient China, the emperor was called the "Son of Heaven". He was seen as the descendant of the god from heaven and carried the divine bloodline. In later dynasties, the title was replaced by the "Son of Dragon". From then on, Chinese people called themselves the descendants of Dragon.

Who was the Dragon that the Chinese people referred to? Are they referring to the dinosaurs that roamed in prehistoric China? Or are they referring to a fearsome god with dragon face and body whom the emperor claimed his divine heritage?

The Book of Revelation says Satan is the Red Dragon that God will hurls into the eternal pit of fire.⁶ The national flag color of China is red. Is the Dragon revered by the Chinese a red dragon? If so, who wants to be the descendants of Red Dragon that God of the Bible will destroy eternally?

Genesis 6:1-4 recorded the fallen angels had come down to earth and mixed with earthly women. Their offspring, the Nephilim, were worshipped as demigods by earthly men for their super strength and great statute. They were the children from the fallen angels who were called the Sons of God. They carried the bloodline of the fallen angels whom ordinary men worshipped as their king, ruler, or emperor.

The Nephilim were the mighty men and renowned men of old in the time of Noah as recorded in the Bible. People who migrated from the biblical land brought their memory of the Nephilim whom they revered as super heroes and divine leader to ancient China. The Nephilim were the paragon of godly and divine leader in ancient time. They were the godly king, ruler, and emperor behind the concept and title of the Son of God or Son of Heaven in China and many ancient cultures.

CHAPTER 6 – VANISHED MONGOLOID RACE

THE TERM "RACE" IS CONFUSING. People generally look at race as a homogenous people who have the same facial and or physical features and skin color. Thus, the white race refers to white skinned European Caucasians; the brown race refers to brown skinned Middle Easterners and darker East Indians; the black race refers to broad nose thick lips Negroes; the red race refers to American Indians and; the yellow race refers to slit eyes yellow skinned Mongoloid people.

People also define race by nationality. Thus, all people in China are Chinese; all people in the United States are Americans and; all people in Canada are Canadians. However, in reality, not all people in China are Mongoloid Chinese and not all people in the United States and Canada are Europeans. Chinese, American, and Canadian are simply the name of people from the same country. Within the country, there can be different ethnic people of diverse racial background who could be Mongoloid, Caucasian, and Negro type of people.

There is no right or wrong in how a person defines race. A race can be defined as the congregation of people as one people under a distinguishable name to represent their collective faith or collective values they believe. For example, the racial name "Jew" is the name for all Jewish people who worshipped the God of the Old Testament and practice the Jewish tradition. Being a Jewish person doesn't mean he or she requires a Jewish nose and brown complexion. Some Jewish people are black people (Ethiopian Jews) and some Jews are Europeans (Polish and Russian Jews). The racial term "Jew" is the name of a people who embraces Judaism and the Jewish way of life. When Hitler persecuted the Jews, he didn't realize he was also murdering Jewish people of European stock. Hitler saw the Jewish race as a homogenous people but he was wrong.

Imagine 1,000 years from now people read the history book about race in China and United States. Immediately, they will associate Mongoloids are the people in China and Europeans are the people in United States. It is natural for future generations to see a homogenous people inhabited in China and in the United States despite diverse races coexisted with the majority type of people in those two countries.

Chinese historians and many Chinese people assumed Mongoloid people were the only people inhabited in China since the beginning of time. When they look back at the legendary and early history of China, they see a Chinese Yellow Emperor, Chinese sages, Chinese primitive people, and Chinese barbarians invading Chinese border from outside of China. Undoubtedly they saw everyone in the beginning time of China was Mongoloid and nobody else. Their view on the homogenous people in early China is like the people in the future who read the history book about race in China and the United States.

I for one believe China had a multi-racial beginning at the dawn of her pre-dynastic history. I believe Mongoloid, Caucasian, and Negro type of people had entered early China by different routes and converged along the fertile Yellow River in the north and the mighty Yangtze River in the south. Separately, they started their own unique culture in northern and southern China. Main cultures found in early China were Yangshao, Longshan, Dawenkou, Daxi, Majiabang, Hemudu, Liangzhu, and Dapenkeng cultures. Each culture had their unique way of life, diet, potteries, and arts. Millet was the main diet in the north and rice was the main diet in the south. Early people at the dawn of China history are not entirely a Mongoloid race.

As early as 60,000 years ago primitive Negroes from Africa had journeyed to the East as far as to Australia and New Zealand. Their route via southern Arabia to India and Southeast Asia would trespass southern China. It would be foolish to say the primitive Africans had missed the vast land of China in their eastward journey and had never stepped a foot in China. Negroes could be the first people to arrive in southern China long before any other races. They could be the primitive people who lived on tree to hide from wild beasts and ate raw nut and meat as described in Chinese legends!

Brown Caucasian people from ancient Near East definitely had wandered to China. They were the first people to transcend the hunter gathering way of life to become nomadic people. The Sumerians were the first people to spark the cradle of civilization in ancient Mesopotamia (ancient Iraq). They had higher knowledge and skills to equip themselves to journey afar to distant lands. The names of legendary Chinese sages such as Fuxi, Nuwa, and Shennong sound Middle Eastern more than Chinese names. Migrants from ancient Near East and Central Asia could be the origin of legendary sages who suddenly appeared and bumped into the primitive Chinese people in Chinese legends!

European Caucasian people had also reached the western edge of China as early as 4,000 years ago. Their blonde hairs, colored eyes, tattooed arms, and dehydrated mummies unearthed in Tarim Basim in Xinjiang shocked historians by their early appearance in the western border of China. Chinese historians can no longer discard the possibility that European Caucasians might had entered and mingled with early Chinese settlers in pre-dynastic China. The barbarians whom the ancient Chinese called Foreign Devils might be part of the population that coexisted with the Mongoloid Chinese at the dawn of Chinese history!

The multi-racial beginning of China is not a fantasy. Images of Mongoloid, Caucasian, and Negro faces could be seen sculpted on potteries, bowls, jars and relics unearthed in various archaeological sites all over China. Their images testified that all types of people had converged and mingled in the beginning of China. The diversity of races in early China inspired the Chinese to call their world "Middle Kingdom".

Chinese people belong to the Mongoloid race. To the readers of the Bible, they can easily identify Caucasian and Negro type of people in the stories of the Bible. For example, readers can identify Israelite, Canaanite, Amorite, Assyrian, and brownish Egyptians were Caucasian people. Readers can also tell the Roman and the Greek were white Caucasian people or European. And everyone knows the Ethiopians and dark Egyptians in the stories of the Bible were Negroes. However, when it comes to the Mongoloid people, it is not easy for readers to identify them from the names and tribes mentioned in the Bible. It seemed the Mongoloid people had vanished from the face of the earth in the Bible.

To the world most populous nation, China inhabited the largest Mongoloid people in the world. Imagine a gospel preacher trying to convince the Chinese people the Bible is the Holy Book for all nations and races. What can the preacher say when being asked where is the evidence of Mongoloid Chinese people in the stories of the Bible? As said above, readers can easily identify Caucasian and Negro type of people in the stories of the Bible, but no one can tell what people mentioned in the Bible are Mongoloids? Although this is not the reason why Chinese people would believe God, however, it is an incredulous rejection by the Chinese people to the Bible's claim for its inclusiveness of all races.

I searched the Bible but found no clear mentioning or even the slightest indication of Mongoloid type of people in the entire 66 books of the Bible. It seemed the Mongoloid people had departed the biblical land long before the authors of the Bible noticed their existence.

Caucasians and Negroes were the common type of people in the early world of the Bible. From Seth to Noah and from Shem to Abraham, the people in the stories of the Old Testament were Middle Eastern brown Caucasians. Negroes were definitely in the picture since Egypt was a flourishing empire where large number of black Egyptians inhabited. We could assume Mongoloid people coexisted with the Caucasians and Negroes in the land of the Bible. However, the Mongoloids must be a shy race or a small minority since no particular people, race or tribe mentioned in the Bible could outstand their existence from the main stream Caucasian and Negro people at that time.

The rise of the Greeks and Romans brought the European Caucasians into Ancient Near East. But there were no particular historical event that could mark the appearance of the Mongoloid people in Ancient Near East until the rise of the Mongols in AD 1162. By that time, the Old Testament had been written over three thousands years and the New Testament had been written for over a thousand years. It was too late for the Mongoloid people to show up to be included in the Bible.

Where were the Mongoloid people in the Bible?

This is a difficult question. We may never find a satisfactory answer to this question. I can only theorize what I imagine might have happened and pray that God whispers inspiration into my ears as I attempt to put forward an answer. I hope readers be gracious to read my theory with an open mind.

I think before and after the Deluge, Mongoloid people in the biblical land are a minority people and don't have an independent tribe of their own. Because of their smaller statue and weaker physical strength, they were subdued by the stronger Caucasian and Negro tribes and forced to live as a subsidiary people. They became an anonymous people living under their host tribe.

Under such circumstances living as second class people, many Mongoloid people chose to depart to other and distant land. This could be why large number of Mongoloids left the biblical land more than the Caucasian and Negro people. Obviously, the Mongoloid people wanted their own independence and freedom; therefore, moving away as far as they could was the ultimate solution. Large number of Mongoloids chose to depart the biblical land. Many headed east as they saw more and more Mongoloids dominated East Asia in that part of the world.

It seemed the Mongoloid people had mixed with Caucasians and Negroes more often than the latter two with each other. As a subsidiary people under their host tribe, Mongcloids became an in-between stock of people for interracial breeding. This increased the diversity of facial and physical traits inherited by the Mongoloids.

Among the three racial types: Caucasian, Negro, and Mongoloid, the Mongoloids have the largest varieties of facial features. From broad nose to little nose, thick lips to one line mouth, big round eyes to slit eyes, bushy beard to long thin beard, and wavy to straight hair, they have them all. The diversity of facial traits among Chinese people first occurred during their intermixing with Caucasian and Negro people before they departed the biblical homeland. And after the

Mongoloid people dominated China, they subdued many races and blended them into the bloodline of the Mongoloids.

In modern China, one can still see the legacy of diversity of facial traits on Chinese faces blossom out of a profound culture of over 5,000 years of history. Most northern Chinese have fair skin, bigger round eyes, narrow nose, and rounder face. While southern Chinese have yellowish skin, broader nose, slanted eyes, and squarer face. Physically, northern Chinese are taller and southern Chinese are shorter with some less than five feet tall. It is clear that Chinese people have diverse ancestral roots.

When Moses recorded the genealogy of Adam to Noah in Genesis 5:3-32 and the genealogy of Shem to Abraham in Genesis 11:10-32, he added that there were other sons and daughters begot by the patriarchs but he couldn't account for their names and numbers. Could some of the other children begot by the patriarchs were of Mongoloid stock?

Furthermore, the Table of Nations recorded by Moses in Genesis 10:1-32, all the names of the tribes and nations mentioned were obviously of Middle Eastern region origin where Noah's three sons: Shem, Japheth, and Ham inhabited before their descendants spread out to repopulate the world. Among the names mentioned, Bible scholars suspect one of the tribes from the sons of Canaan called "Sinites" to be the forefather of the Mongoloid

Chinese people. There was not much information in ancient documents about the Sinites. They seemed to worship the moon god "Sin" and their tribe name could be the origin of the Latin name "Sino" to denote things related to China.

If the Sinites were purely a Mongoloid race, then Canaan, youngest son of Ham, would be a Mongoloid and bred with a Mongoloid woman. However, the Canaanites were obviously a brown Caucasian people more than a Negro or Mongoloid people. Therefore, the Sinites couldn't be an entirely Mongoloid people. This leaves us with the only conclusion and that is part of the population of the Sinites are Mongoloid people. Perhaps the ratio of Mongoloid people in the Sinite tribe was significantly high to the point where they were identified as a Mongoloid tribe more than a Canaanite Caucasian tribe.

As suggested earlier, due to the inferior size and strength of the Mongoloid people, they were subdued by the Caucasian and Negro people to live as a subsidiary people in their tribes. The status of the Mongoloid Sinites was the closest Mongoloid people could get recognized as a significant people in the biblical land.

The lack of visibility of the Mongoloid people in the Bible was due to their small number remained in the biblical land after their mass departure to distant land. Thus, the authors of the 66 books of the Bible had little or no information about them.

The Mongoloid race is the largest race on earth where majority of them live in China. The origin of the Mongoloid Chinese is a mystery and the beginning history of China can only be explained by legends. What is the chance that the invisibility of Mongoloid people in the entire 66 books of the Bible is the clue to the origin of the Chinese in China?

The missing Mongoloids in the Bible had fled to China where they restarted their lives as an independent people far away from the stronger Caucasian and Negro people who subdued them. After a long period of isolation in China, the Mongoloids had totally forgotten their ancestral root in the biblical land. Perhaps it was the plan of God to separate them in the East for future revelation of His blessing to the Chinese people.

CHAPTER 7 - TOWER OF BABEL

Genesis 11:1-8 tells us that God divided and scattered mankind all over the earth by confused their language. Mankind was forced to divide and regroup by language so that people could understand each other. Hundreds if not thousands of language groups were formed. They were forced to leave and find new home in new land away from the biblical land. For those groups that scattered to the East, they reached China after overcame long stretches of rough and treacherous terrains covering deserts, mountains, steppes, tundra, and river.

The Tower of Babel is the most profound event in the Bible which forever divided mankind up to this date. Thousands of languages were formed, thus, thousands of unique people speaking their own language saw each other as aliens. Race was no longer a matter of skin color. If you couldn't speak the language, you were not one of us. This was the new criteria to be part of the tribe and nation formed by language in the post Tower of Babel world.

The effect of the division by language changed the racial composition of the language group formed. After the Tower of Babel, the divided language groups were less and less a homogenous people. Because God divided mankind by language and not by racial type, the possibility of mixed races within each group was certain. Therefore, Caucasians, Mongoloids, and Negroes could be found within each language group who spoke the same language.

After the Tower of Babel, it was natural for the newly formed language groups with majority of one racial type to move to their original racial homeland. For example, white Caucasians would scatter to Northern and Western Europe since they were more concentrated there. The brown Caucasians scattered all over ancient Near East, Central Asia, and the Indian subcontinent. The Mongoloids scattered to the Far East since their ancestors had departed the biblical land and established in China long before Nimrod ruled the world. Therefore, Mongoloids were the dominant race in East Asia; white Caucasians dominated Europe and the brown Caucasians dominated ancient Near East all the way to Central Asia and India. The black people retreated to Africa where their remote ancestors in the days of Eden enjoyed a utopia there.

Ancient Chinese documents recorded the Mongols, a vicious enemy of the Chinese, were a color eyed people. How could that be? If the Mongols were Mongoloid type of people, they should have brown to dark eyeballs and hairs. Clearly, what the ancient Chinese saw were not a pure blooded Mongols. After the Tower of Babel, the language group which formed the forefathers of the

Mongols must be a heterogeneous people. In fact, ancient history recorded mixed people of Caucasian and Mongoloid barbarians roamed the Steppes from Central Asia to Mongolia. They were the notorious savages abhorred and hated by ancient civilized people in the East and West. In the East, they were called the Xiongnu by the Chinese and in the West they were called the Hun. The Xiongnu was mostly Mongoloids and the Hun was mostly Caucasians.

The Eurasia Steppes is truly the land of heterogeneous races. This vast stretch of geography was once the corridor of horror in the days of the Tower of Babel where the newly formed diverse language groups scattered in fear. Today mixed people of Caucasians and Mongoloids coexisted from Turkey all the way to the former Soviet Union eastern states (Kazakhstan, Uzbekistan, Turkmenistan, Kyrgyzstan, and Tajikistan). The legacy of heterogeneous people after the Tower of Babel continues today under nations of mixed Caucasian and Asiatic people who thrive in this region.

From Europe to India subcontinent, Indo-European language testified that mankind once spoke a common language before they split into different language groups.² After the Tower of Babel, the family tree of Indo-Europeans scattered all over Europe, Asia Minor, Central to Southwest Asia and the Indian Continent. Who could imagine English,

German, Italian, Hindi, Punjabi, Spanish, French, Russian, Bengali, Iranian, and other Indo-European languages were once a common language? Indo-European language groups formed after the Tower of Babel must be composed of mixed racial types of people before they split up again to form their own tribe and nation.

In ancient Egypt, evidence of heterogeneous races appeared in paintings on the wall of ancient Egyptian palaces and tombs. White, brown, black, and yellow people converged in this ancient great land of the Nile. It seemed the black people in Africa were easily enslaved and ruled by foreign people despite of their majority advantage. To the eyes of historians, the image of ancient Egypt was more brown than black.

In the most western province of China, mixed race of Uyghur and Chinese coexisted in the Xinjiang Uyghur Autonomous Region. This unique brand of Chinese nationalities is a new breed of Chinese who carry both Caucasian and Mongoloid blood.

After the Tower of Babel, the language groups that scattered to the Far East had brought Caucasian and Negro people to China. They were minority in the language groups where the Mongoloids dominated in number. Images of Caucasians and Negroes can be seen sculpted on ancient potteries and jars unearthed in China.

After the inception of the Shang Dynasty (1,766 - 1,050 BC), the Mongoloids became master of China. From then onwards, the number of Caucasians and Negroes declined year after year. Their descendants gradually mixed and blended into the Chinese bloodline.

In modern China, 93% of the population is Han Chinese (regarded as the pure Chinese stock) and the rest is composed of 55 other ethnic people such as Uyghur, Mongolian, Korean, and even Russian. Chinese people are culturally united by Chinese writing. Accredit to 5,000 years of continuation of Chinese culture and tradition, most of the minority ethnic people in China have assimilated the Chinese way of life and thinking. However, beneath China cultural shell, many ethnic traditions and beliefs are still non-Chinese.

The Table of Nations in Genesis 10:1-32 listed all the known descendants of Shem, Japheth, and Ham by tribe. The names of the tribes and nations had to be recorded after the Tower of Babel because the descendants of Noah's three sons formed their own tribe and nation according to their own tongue (by language). Therefore, the descendants of Shem, Japheth, and Ham had already spoken different languages in the post Tower of Babel world.

The Tower of Babel incident could explain why Bible scholars had a hard time to pinpoint the racial type of the tribes and nations formed by the descendants of Shem, Japheth, and Ham. The conventional perception by Bible scholars is that Black people (Negroes) and East Asians (Mongoloids) are the descendants of Ham; Brown and dark Caucasians the descendants of Shem and; White Caucasians or Europeans the descendants of Japheth.

For whatever genetic abnormity, Ham's descendants diverse into two separate races: Negroes and Mongoloids; while Shem and Japheth's descendants produced only Caucasian people. Was Ham a carrier of two types of Y Chromosomes or his descendants mutated more vigorously than those of Shem and Japheth? Of course, it was neither of the cases.

As said early in the chapter, God separated mankind by language and not by racial type or skin color. This means that every language groups formed after the Tower of Babel would compose a mixed people of Caucasians, Negroes, and Mongoloids. Every language group formed would have a dominant race who could be Caucasians, Negroes, or Mongoloids. Therefore, the minority races were invisible because of their small number.

For example, a language group might have 80% Negroes and the rest of the 20% Caucasian and Mongoloids. To outsiders this group would be seen as a Negro people despite there were 20% non-Negroes. Other groups might have 80% Mongoloids and 20% mixed of Caucasians and Negroes. Such groups would be seen as a Mongoloid people by outsiders. There must be many racial mixed groups formed which later led to their descendants produced mixed children with some appeared like their father or mother's race. This was how Ham descendants acquired two racial lineages: the Blacks and East Asians, perhaps, due to their number increased more than the descendants of Shem and Japheth.

Western Bible scholars prefer racial homogeneity in the biblical roots of races. Western Bible scholars are not fond of the idea of mixed races in the lineage of the descendants of Shem, Japheth, and Ham. They want clear cut racial purity to separate races. They want white and brown people to be in the line of Shem and Japheth, and the Black and East Asian people in the line of Ham. Although this is not racism, it could undermine the divine plan of God for mankind to live as a mixed race.

God is no racist. He is a fair God. The division of mankind by language was the fairest way to divide mankind. God wants to prevent the danger of world domination by a united homogenous people. Adolf Hitler had tried it and ended in total destruction. Beware of the European Economic Community (EEC) to be the next united homogenous people to challenge God's plan for mankind.

The Book of Revelation tells us that mankind will be ruled by the leader of the Anti-Christ in the end time. Mankind will be led by an evil ruler to challenge God like Nimrod did. This time is not about constructing a tower to reach heaven. This time is the final duel between good and evil!

CHAPTER 8 - SAGES

CHINESE LEGENDS SAID THERE WERE FIVE SAGES appeared to the early Chinese people and taught them essential survival skills.[1] From anthropological timeline, I would put the five sages appeared near the end of the Paleolithic period and the beginning of the Neolithic period (10000 BC to 4000 BC). This was the period where Paleolithic and Neolithic humans existed in parallel timeframe where some humans were very backward and some humans had crossed the threshold of Neolithic era. During this period of time, diverse levels of intelligence of primitive people scattered all over the world.

The first sage, Youchao (Have Nest), suddenly appeared out of nowhere in China. He taught the primitive Chinese people how to build shelter on tree. Then came Suiren (Fire Maker), he taught people how to make fire. Then Fuxi (Animal Domesticator) arrived, he taught people how to domesticate cattle and make tools. His wife Nuwa taught people how to harvest silk from cocoon. Finally, Shennong (Divine Husbandman) appeared, he taught people how to cultivate crops and use herbs for medicine.

The first two sages, Youchao and Suiren, probably appeared to the primitive Chinese people as early as 10000 BC to 6000 BC. During this time,

Youchao and Suiren had mastered the skill of hut building and making fire. Youchao must come from a place where his people were skilled builders of primitive shelter with mammoth bones, tree branches, or clay covered by straws or animal skin. Suiren came from a place where his people were masters of fire making for their everyday cooking, heat, and even as weapon to scare attacking wild beasts.

Sage Youchao and Suiren could come from northern China where it was populated by a heterogeneous people comprising of Mongoloids and Caucasians. Youchao and Suiren could be a Mongoloid, a Caucasian or a mixed breed. Both wandered south and were astonished to discover the backwardness of the primitive Chinese people.

Both Youchao and Suiren came from their homeland where people had mastered the basic skills of survival. Both sages must be shock to see the pitiful Chinese living in fear on tree and eating uncooked meat and raw nuts.

Fuxi, Nuwa (Fuxi's wife), and Shennong appeared to the early Chinese people long after Youchao and Suiren died. I would put their time of appearance around 5000 BC to 4000 BC. They brought Neolithic knowledge such as domestication of cattle, tool making, silk farming, agriculture, and herbs for medicine to the early Chinese people. Fuxi is also said to be the inventor of "I-Ching" which is regarded as the first form of Chinese writing.

By the time Fuxi, Nuwa, and Shennong appeared to the primitive Chinese people, they were no longer a savage people living on tree; they lived in huts in simple settlement and had mastered fire for cooking and heat. During this period of time in ancient Near East, organized settlement (even city), agriculture, animal husbandry, herbal medicine, writing, pottery making, and silk weaving had spread to Egypt, Europe, Anatolia (in Turkey), and Central Asia. By 4000 BC, Sumer was the first complex and advanced civilization in the world. During this time, increasing nomads from outside of China converged along the Yellow River from west to east. The growing diversity of people in China began to shape her into an expanding world of "Middle Kingdom".

The early Chinese called their land "Middle Kingdom" not because they thought they were a superior people. They called it so because of the presence of diversity of races (white, yellow, brown, black, and even red skinned people) converging along the mighty Yellow River. Their feeling was similar to modern people living in big city in North America where many races mingled in a multi-ethnic world.

The above five sages appeared in China out of nowhere over an unknown period of time, and laid the foundation for the primitive Chinese people to rise to a civilized people. Although the sages were legendary figures, however, their appearances were very significant events in the prehistory of China. If they didn't appeared, the pathetic primitive Chinese people could face extinction and vanish from the land of China.

Other Chinese legends also said early China was ruled by Three Sovereigns and Five Emperors in the remote past.[3] No one is certain when this remote past was. Time in Chinese legends is anyone guesses. The Five Emperors were believed to be the above five sages that appeared in early China out of nowhere.

The Three Sovereigns were generally referred to as the Emperor of Heaven, the Emperor of Earth, and the Emperor of Land. Like the mysterious sages, Chinese historians don't know if the Three Sovereigns were real or not, and they have no clue to who these mysterious figures were. However, judging from their title, it seemed to suggest that they might be some kind of deities or gods. Thus, the reference of the first Sovereign Emperor, the Emperor of Heaven, would likely be the Supreme God; the second and third Sovereign Emperor would be his left and right hand delegates in the heavenly world.

Where did Chinese legends get the idea of the Divine Trinity of the Three Sovereign Emperors? Why didn't they come up with two, four, seven or any other number of sovereign emperors? Why three? Three is the number of Christian Trinity of the Father, the Son, and the Holy Spirit. They are indeed the Sovereign Rulers of Heaven and Earth. The odd number three couldn't be just a whimsical number picked out by some wise Chinese story tellers to create legends for their posterity. The concept of the Trinity of the Three Sovereign Emperors must be borrowed from religious idea that was introduced to the early Chinese people from the outside world.

China has never been a birth place of religion. From the dawn of Chinese history till the present day, China remains to be a seeker of other people's faith. Buddhism, Hinduism, Islam, and Christianity are all imported religions to China. Confucianism and Taoism are not really a religion. Both are profound esoteric philosophy more than the preaching of godly doctrine. Confucius and Lao Tse never advocated their teachings as a religious teaching. Their followers were students seeking knowledge of humanity and higher truth. In this respect, the concept of Trinity couldn't be an indigenous idea invented by early Chinese people.

Of all the religious scriptures in the world, only the Bible professes the Holy Trinity of God. Therefore, only believers of this Trinity would be the ones to bring the concept of Holy Trinity to

China. Could these believers of Christian Trinity of God be the other children and their descendants form the line of Seth and Shem that had migrated to China? Could they be the ones who seeded the concept of the Holy Trinity to the early Chinese people?

Chinese historians had no way to verify if the legendary figures in the beginning history of China were real or not. It is up to the individual Chinese to determine if he or she believes it or not. If he or she believes the legends as history of China's past, then the Three Sovereigns and the Five Emperors were credible historical figures; if he or she discards the legends as pure fantasy, then all the legendary figures in the beginning history of China were fictional characters created by imaginative Chinese story tellers.

Chinese legends said the five sages appeared to the inferior Chinese people as a mortal human being. Some myths said Fuxi and Nuwa's lower body was a snake and Shennong had a human body and the head of an ox.[4] Although some of the sages were described as having a hybrid human and animal body; however, all of them were not worshipped as god by the early Chinese people and no religion was formed after them.

The description of Chinese mythical figures with hybrid human and animal body in Chinese folklores and myths might not be just pure fantasy.

The ancient Celtic people were renowned for their arms and body tattoos with motifs and horrified images of wild beast.⁵ A person with whole or part of the body tattooed as scales of a snake or wild beast would leave a terrified memory to the people who got scared. Could the description of the half human and half creature body of the sages were people who practiced the Celtic tattoo tradition? If so, could the sages come from a branch of the Celtic nomadic tribe or come from a people influenced by the Celtic tradition?

The Celtic tradition of tattooing the face and body spread East and West across the Eurasia continent for at least 4,000 years. The 4,000 years old European mummies unearthed in Tarim Basin in western China had heavy tattoos on their face and arms. They were irrefutable evidences of European Caucasian people who practiced Celtic tattooing and had penetrated deep into the western border of China.

The European mummies unearthed in Tarim Basin undoubtedly proved that ancient Europeans had entered China as early as 4,000 years ago and they might have mingled with the Mongoloid people. Furthermore, we couldn't rule out these European Caucasians might have influenced the early Chinese people with higher knowledge in agriculture and tool making skills.

These European mummies died around the time of legendary period of the Yellow Emperor (2800 BC) and the Xia dynasty (2200-1766 BC). What if these European migrants were part of Yellow Emperor subjects and assisted him to unify all the other tribes in northern China? What if Yellow Emperor himself was from one of the clans of the European Caucasians? Could the title "Yellow" is referring to the color of Yellow Emperor's hairs (blonde hair) rather than referred to the abundant yellow loess along the Yellow River or referred to the Yellow River itself?

Of course, the above notions defy conventional thinking of Yellow Emperor as a Mongoloid Chinese. But the argument against Yellow Emperor as a non-Mongoloid is equally fragile as no one can be sure if the first Chinese people were a homogenous Mongoloid people or not. What if the first Chinese people were not a homogenous Mongoloid people? Can we be certain that since the dawn of China, only Mongoloid people inhabited the land?

Early Chinese documents recorded that there were other tribes entered China since the dawn of Chinese history.[6] These aliens were often seen as derogatory foreign barbarians and foreign devils. They caused so much troubles to China that after Emperor Shih Huang Ti conquered all of China (221 BC), he commenced the erection of the Great Wall that stretched 4,000 miles from Heilongjiang

Province in northeastern China to the desert region of Gansu Province in the northwest. The evidence of multi-races at the dawn of China is hard to dismiss. Perhaps European Caucasians in early China were invisible because of their small number in the dominant world of Mongoloids.

Were the sages Mongoloid?

The sages in Chinese legends were non-Chinese who came from outside of China. They came from an advanced culture while Chinese people were still in the state of dire primitiveness. The sages had to come from an advance culture because they possessed higher knowledge that was not known by the primitive Chinese. Also, the sages couldn't be the children of the primitive Chinese because if they were, they had to be born a prodigy in order to be smarter than their own people.

Furthermore, the sages had to acquire knowledge of their trade in a higher culture before they were capable to teach the primitive Chinese people. Where would this advance culture be? It couldn't be in China because if it were, the early Chinese people wouldn't be so primitive. So it had to be outside of China.

Mankind's first civilization arose in ancient Mesopotamia in ancient Near East. There in the land of Sumer, the Sumerian were the first people to develop organized settlement, agriculture, domestication of cattle, weaving clothes, pottery making, metallurgy, use of wheels, writing, astronomy, and public administration system long before anyone else did. If anyone wanted to learn any of the above trade, he or she had to live and practice there. This region of the world had to be the place where the sages had learnt and mastered their trade because there was no other place on earth more advanced than the first cradle of civilization of mankind. This was the region where Caucasian people concentrated in the world. The sages who wandered into China could be Caucasian!

The sages displayed great leadership and administration skill which further added credibility to their origin from ancient Near East where the system of law and order and government was born. Sage Fuxi and Sage Nuwa were definitely a leader where early Chinese people looked up to them for guidance and leadership. Sage Shennong became a tribal emperor and earned the title of "Flame Emperor" for teaching people how to clear the land by fire before cultivating crops. He also incepted the earliest tribal kingdom called the "Yin Dynasty". Legends said Shennong ruled over many tribal princes in northern China near Inner Mongolia. After he died, his successors continued to carry the title of "Flame Emperor".

Around 2800 BC the last Flame Emperor clashed with Yellow Emperor for supremacy of northern China but was defeated.[1] In the south, Yellow Emperor crushed his arch enemy "Chiyou", the leader of the Man tribe. Thereafter, Yellow Emperor became the undisputed Tribal Emperor of early China.[7]

All primitive people were superstitious in one way or another. Primitive people were easily terrified by wild beasts, thunder, lightening, storm, wild fire, earthquake, volcano eruption, and all kinds of natural disasters. Out of fear they worshipped any natural and supernatural power that could destroy them. Fear was the trigger to superstition and worship of object, idol, nature, and wise men by primitive people. However, it was unusual for the primitive Chinese people to have no godly feeling for the sages. They never worshipped the sages as gods. All they saw the sages were a flesh and blood mortal being like them and nothing more. It was obvious that the encounters between the sages and the primitive Chinese people were a human to human contact between an advanced people and an inferior people.

When the Spanish expedition force of the 16th Century landed in South America with their guns and canons, they were worshipped as gods by the Mayans who believed the Spanish were their ancestral white gods whom they had been waiting for.[8] The Spanish invaders took advantage of the ignorance of the Mayans and enslaved them to exploit their vast amount of gold treasure. The greediness and immorality of the Spanish destroyed the Mayan culture.

The sages who appeared to the primitive Chinese people didn't pretend to be a god. They could seize the opportunity to frighten and enslaved the primitive Chinese people for gains like the Spanish did to the Mayans. Instead the sages were very kind and gracious to help and teach a very backward people. In this respect, the sages were a benevolent person. The sages were surprisingly kind and generous in a still savage world at the dawn of China. Perhaps the sages were religious people. Perhaps the sages were believers of a loving and caring God so they had agape love for the primitive Chinese people. The sages could be from the line of Seth and Shem who practiced the faith of love and virtue.

Western historians have always suspected the rise of Chinese civilization is a result of diffusion of knowledge from ancient Near East. Chinese historians strongly argue the origin of Chinese civilization was an indigenous event with no outside influence. However, mankind's first civilization arose in ancient Near East almost two thousands years earlier than China. How could we discard the possibility that advanced people in ancient Near East had not traveled and made contact with early people in China?

The fact is distance is no obstacle to the spreading of knowledge. It is a matter of time. History repeatedly confirmed that advanced culture could always impart knowledge to inferior culture because the former has the power to influence the latter. We see this in modern time where advanced technology in the West reached the East whether the latter likes it or not. Since the dawn of mankind, human beings roamed all over the world and spread knowledge to where they went. It is just a matter of time before higher knowledge replaces the antiquated ones through human contact.

The rise of Chinese civilization will always be a subject of scrutiny as long as the beginning history of China hinges on legends.

CHAPTER 9 - PRIMITIVE CHINESE PEOPLE

CHINESE LEGENDS said the earliest Chinese people were a very primitive people. They lived on trees to hide from wild beasts and they ate raw meat and nuts because they had no knowledge of how to make fire. The condition of their living would put them existed in the dawn of mankind where humans lived like animals. The primitive Chinese people in the legends were inferior to the Paleolithic people who had mastered fire and knew how to build simple hut shelter.

The primitive Chinese lived on tree and ate raw food when sage Youchao and Suiren appeared. This suggested that they wouldn't be living in a cold and frigid region. The primitive Chinese people must be in total nakedness or in minimum coverage by leaves as they couldn't dare to kill wild animals for skins for clothing.

A year round tropical or sub-tropical place in southern China would enable the primitive Chinese people to stay naked without the threat of cold weather which they would surely freeze to death. After the last Ice Age ended (12,000 to 10,000 years ago), moderate and warm climate prevailed in southern China. If the primitive Chinese could only survive in a warm climate, southern China would likely be the region where Youchao and Suiren encountered the primitive Chinese people.

The primitive Chinese people in the legend might be African Negroes or descendants of African Negroes that had migrated out of Africa to the Far East. They were the first prehistoric humans to wander out of Africa around 60,000 years ago and journeyed East. Archaeological and genetic evidences strongly suggested that prehistoric Africans had left colonies in Southeast Asia, Australia, and New Zealand. They moved out of Africa and traveled in a southerly route near the coast of Arabia and India all the way to Asia.

The facial traits of African Negroes can be seen on the aboriginals in Australia and New Zealand. They resemble their ancestor Negro's wide and broad nose and thick lips. In Southeast Asia, the traits of Negro's nose and lips are also visible in many Southeast Asians although they appear in various sizes. Many southern Chinese also have broad nose and medium to thick lips. They could be descendants of early mixed Mongoloids and Negroes.

This might sound far fetch. Northern and southern Chinese people don't look alike at all. One can tell the obvious facial and physical difference between northern Chinese and southern Chinese. The average northerners are tall with long and narrow nose and fair skin; the average southerners are short with wide and broad nose and yellowish to brownish skin.

The remote forefathers of the northern Chinese are true Mongoloid originated from a common and remote ancestry of the American Indian, Siberian, Mongolian, Tibetan, Korean, and Japanese.² The remote forefathers of the southern Chinese are a people of mixed Mongoloid and prehistoric African Negroes.

Were the first people to arrive in southern China African Negro? Were they the primitive Chinese people described by the Chinese legend that lived on trees and ate uncooked raw food?

We can't discard such possibilities. Prehistoric Africans that migrated out of Africa around 60,000 years ago wouldn't miss the vast land of southern China in their eastward journey. If they could reach afar to Australia and New Zealand, they would also reach southern China as well. Not all Africans would head south to the Pacific coastline to Indonesia, Australia, and New Zealand. There had to be others that continued their journey eastward and entered southern China.

The primitive Chinese people in the Chinese legend could be descendants of Prehistoric Africans that had settled in southern China. They continued to live in primitive way until Youchao and Suiren encountered them. They could be the first people to arrive in southern China and preceded the arrival of the Mongoloid people.

After Youchao and Suiren appeared and taught the primitive Chinese people basic survival skill, their level of intelligence was raised by the knowledge gained from the two sages despite they were still backward. God must be kind to the primitive Chinese people because three more sages would arrive to be the catalyst of their ultimate transcendence to a civilized people.

The first Neolithic culture, Yangshao Culture, appeared in China during this period of time. Yangshao Culture thrived in the west of Yellow River around 4500 BC and spread towards the east. The famous Yangshao site was unearthed in Banpo in the upper and middle Yellow River in Xian, Henan province. It was an organized settlement covering an area of 10,000 square meters. It is dated to be around 4000 BC. This is the earliest Neolithic culture found in China.

From the relics and potteries unearthed in Banpo, archaeologists believed the Yangshao people were a highly skilled people. They made colorful potteries resembled the shapes that flourished in Central Asia and the Near East. Yangshao people also had great artistic skills. Their arts are vividly depicted by motifs, geometrical patterns, and symbols on potteries, bowls, and jars. Yangshao was China's first Neolithic culture.

Sage Fuxi, Nuwa, and Shennong had to be the earliest Neolithic people to appear in China before

Yangshao culture developed in China. The people of Yangshao were a very organized people living in a very organized settlement. Their level of skills in fishing, farming, and making potteries could make everyone of them a sage to the primitive Chinese people. Therefore, if Fuxi, Nuwa, and Shennong existed in the same era of the Yangshao people, they wouldn't be accredited for the only sages to advance the development of the Chinese people.

Legend said Fuxi invented many tools to improve the way of life of the Chinese people before anybody else. He developed the first version of I-Ching to help people make decision by prediction.[4] His wife, Nuwa, was the first person to teach people how to farm silk and use it to weave clothing. And Shennong was the first sage to teach Chinese people agriculture. He taught people how to prepare and plough field for planting crops. Also, he was an herbalist and tested hundreds of herbs for medicine. Legend said that he got poisoned many times everyday.

Fuxi, Nuwa, and Shennong came and taught early Chinese people things they had no knowledge of but essentials to transform them into a civilized people. Therefore, they had to appear before the rise of Yangshao culture. Perhaps it was the other way round; Yangshao people were the beneficiaries of knowledge passed down from Fuxi, Nuwa, and

Shennong who led early Chinese people to cross the threshold of Neolithic era.

Were Fuxi, Nuwa, and Shennong a Mongoloid Chinese?

Again, we should be open mind that all above three sages might not be a Mongoloid Chinese. They could be a Caucasian or a mixed Caucasian and Mongoloid. We shouldn't assume all legendary figures in Chinese legend were Mongoloids simply because their stories happened in China. The forefathers of all Chinese legendary figures could be non-Mongoloids who had migrated to China and later became part of the heterogeneous people in pre-Dynastic China. Fuxi, Nuwa, and Shennong could be foreigners who came from outside of China. They were smarter, thus, they couldn't be from the same race of the early Chinese people; otherwise they would be born prodigy from a backward people.

The fact that the rise of Chinese civilization arose in the north rather than the south suggested that northern Chinese were influenced by other advanced cultures quicker than the southern Chinese. The infusion of outside knowledge into China from a higher culture helped to expedite the rise of Chinese civilization. And the infusion started from the appearance of the five sages.

Primitive Chinese people in Chinese legends were saved by the five legendary sages. The blessing of sages in the legendary age of China might have a connection with ancient Near East where wanderers including the other sons and daughters from the line of Seth and Shem in Genesis 5: 1-32 and 11:10-26 came from.

After the appearance of the five sages, early Chinese people were on their way to developing one of the magnificent civilizations in the ancient world.

CHAPTER 10 - SHANG-TI

EARLY CIVILIZATIONS worshipped a supreme god who created everything. The Sumerian had Enil; the Egyptians had Atum; the Babylonians had Marduk and; the Hindu had Vishnu, but for the Chinese they had only mere mortal sages and Yellow Emperor.

Right from the dawn of China, Chinese people had little interest in worshipping any gods. However, that doesn't mean the Chinese are not religious people. The word "Religion" can be interchanged with the word "Superstition" in the Chinese interpretation of the supernatural. To the Chinese, ancestral worship is more important than bowing to any gods whom they had no relationship with. Chinese people believe the ghosts of their ancestor and parents can protect them. In many Chinese homes, a shrine is set up where one or more tablet(s) marked with ancestral names is placed for the family to burn incense and offer wine and food to their ancestor. The gods of Chinese family is their ancestor.

Shamanism and ancestral worship were common practices by Chinese people. Each family has a personalized belief that the ghosts of their deceased ancestors are watching and protecting them. This kind of belief is rooted from nomadic shamanism where ancient nomads traveled in family unit cried out to their ancestral spirit for guidance and assistance.

The remote ancestors of the American Indians were vehement practitioners of Shamanism. Siberian, northern Chinese, Mongolian, Korean, and Japanese shared a common remote ancestry with the American Indians. Their remote ancestors were Asiatic nomads that had migrated to East Asia from the biblical land. Paleo-Siberians were the first Proto-Mongoloid people to step foot in Siberia around 18,000 years ago. Not all of them crossed the Bering Strait to Alaska. Some of them stayed in Siberia and some spread all over Northwest Asia. Paleo-Siberians had diversified into different Mongoloid people in Mongolia, Korea, Japan, and China. Shamanism and ancestral worship were the common heritage passed down to the Siberians, Mongolians, Koreans, Japanese, and Chinese from their remote nomadic ancestors.

From the era of Yellow Emperor (2697-2205 BC) to the Xia Dynasty (2205-1766 BC), early Chinese people had no collective religion and had no specific deities whom they collectively worshipped. The Xia people worshipped all kinds of ghosts, spirits, and mountains. In some myths, Yellow Emperor was even said to be the king of all gods himself.

Across the still raw Chinese land, clans and tribes worshipped their own deceased ancestor for protection from the supernatural world. Then suddenly out of nowhere arose a supreme deity called "Shang-Ti". He was revered as the Lord on High who ruled the heavenly kingdom. He endorsed the earthly emperor with the mandate of heaven for ruling the earthly kingdom. This mysterious Lord on High was seen as the supreme deity where rain and storm, life and death, good harvests and natural disasters were blessings and curses from him.[2] Who was this almighty Lord?

The term "Lord" was originated from the land of the Bible where early mankind knew God. After Adam and Eve committed the original sin, mankind lived in the dark without God. In Genesis 4:25, all men begun to call the name of the Lord again after Seth begot Enos. It was at this time that mankind re-acknowledged God as the Lord and called upon Him for help and needs. Early Chinese people couldn't invent the term "Lord" on their own without a monotheistic religion. It had to be an imported idea from outside of China. And it had to come from the biblical land.

The promoter of Shang-Ti was by a people called "Shang". They were an influential clan under the rule of the Xia Dynasty.[3] They were also the ones who overthrown the last Xia emperor to establish their own Shang Dynasty. Ancient Chinese records had no mentioning of the origin of the Shang people. From biblical perspective, their remote ancestors were from the biblical land just like everybody else where the origin of mankind begun. After they arrived in China, the Shang people settled along the Yellow River in Henan province.

The founder of the Shang Dynasty was Tang. His father was Xie who was the son of Emperor Di Ku's second wife (he had 4 wives). Di Ku was one of the successors to the throne of Yellow Emperor.[4] Thus, Tang was of a royal line of the Yellow Emperor.

Shang-Ti was a tribal god of the Shang people before they overthrown the last Xia emperor. After Tang incepted the Shang Dynasty, Shang-Ti became a State god and was worshipped by the Shang Emperor and his high priests.[5]

Who was Shang-Ti? The Shang people didn't elaborate who their supreme deity was. There was no image, no statue, no beautiful songs, and no amazing stories to praise Shang-Ti openly by the Shang people. They even didn't have a name for their supreme god!

The name "Shang-Ti" means "Heavenly Emperor". It was an anonymous title. Like the God of the Bible who replied to Moses when being asked His name, "I am who I am";[6] the name "Shang-Ti" echoed the nameless god of Moses. What a coincidence that the Shang people worshipped a supreme god with no personalized name like the Israelites thousands of miles away in ancient Near East?

In the still untamed and contagious world of shamanism, animism, and ancestral worship in early China, how did the Shang people come up with such daring idea of a supreme deity above all other gods and ancestral ghosts? The Israelites didn't invent monotheism by themselves. God had to convince Abraham to accept Him as the one true God in order to re-establish monotheism in His chosen people. How did the Shang people invent monotheism on their own?

Furthermore, the Shang people mysteriously obeyed Shang-Ti absolutely. In the Book of History (one of earliest ancient documents in China) recorded that Tang (the founder of the Shang Dynasty) issued a declaration of war against Jie, the last and ruthless emperor of the Xia Dynasty.[7] In an emotional speech to his people, Tang said he was ordered by Shang-Ti to overthrow Jie. Since he was afraid of Shang-Ti, he dared not disobey him! Why did Tang have to evoke the supreme authority of Shang-Ti to rally the support of his people? Why did the Shang people have to obey Shang-Ti?

There is only one possible conclusion to the absolute obedience of the Shang people to Shang-Ti:

Shang-Ti had to be a highly revered ancestral god whom the Shang people worshipped generation after generation; if not, why would the Shang people care and listen to Tang evoked Shang-Ti for their support. It seemed the belief of Shang-Ti was a traditional faith passed down to the Shang people like Christian parents passed down their faith to their children. The Shang people were acquainted with Shang-Ti like Christian sons and daughters knew Jesus Christ was their family God. Shang-Ti was the ancestral god of the Shang people for a long time.

The bottom line question is how did the Shang people invent Shang-Ti? I think they didn't. I think the ancestors of the Shang people came from the line of Shem who migrated to China. The children and descendants of Shem were faithful believers of Yahweh. They carried their monotheistic faith to everywhere they went. Yahweh was their ancestral God and they passed down their faith to their descendants who became the Shang people in early China. This was how the Shang people inherited Shang-Ti as their ancestral god. Shang-Ti was their family god.

The Shang people were not entirely a monotheistic people devoted to Shang-Ti. They put Shang-Ti on top of their hierarchy of beliefs. They also practiced ancestral worship and oracle bones foretelling by heating tortoise shell or bone of animals, then observed the cracked lines to predict favorable or unfavorable event. Oracle bones were first unearthed in Xiaotun Village, northwest of Anyang County in Henan. Thousands of oracle bones were later unearthed in various sites and provided historians with much information about the Shang people. Despite of their corruption of faith with other superstitious beliefs, they were loyal worshippers of Shang-Ti.

The Shang Dynasty lasted 644 years (1766-1122 BC). During that period the Shang Dynasty had changed their dynastic name to "Yin" but people continued to call "Shang" as the main dynastic name. Shang Dynasty was overthrown in 1122 BC by the Zhou people who flourished in western China.

The Zhou Dynasty last from 1122 BC to 255 BC. In early period of Zhou Dynasty, Shang-Ti and the Mandate of Heaven continued to be revered by Zhou Emperors and his people. Unfortunately, after several years of hard famine, droughts, and natural disasters, the Zhou people began to doubt the benevolence of Shang-Ti. Eventually, they concluded that Shang-Ti was unreliable and failed to take care of the Zhou people. Gradually, they replaced Shang-Ti with generalized name like "Sky" or "Firmament" making Shang-Ti an impersonal god. It was the beginning of atheism in China.

Although we might never find any evidence that the Shang people were children and descendants from the line of Shem, however, no one could deny that the Shang people embraced monotheism surprisingly in such an early time in China. Monotheism was originated from the land of the Bible, so how could the Shang people invent Shang-Ti if they had no connection with the outside world?

What are the chances that the God of the Bible is actually Shang-Ti whom the Shang people had the highest reverence?

CHAPTER 11 - VIRTUOUS EMPERORS

The legendary period in the beginning history of China appeared a handful of exceptional men of virtues. They were Yao, Shun, and Yu.[1] All three men were later nominated to be emperor for their virtuous character. Yao and Shun became emperor of the Yellow Emperor tribal dynasty. Yu incepted the Xia dynasty and became the first Xia Emperor.

All three emperors were praised for their exceptional loving kindness in ruling for the people. Yao and Shun were regarded by Confucius as the greatest and virtuous ruler of China. Both men were selfless, righteous, sagacious, humble, and diligent in serving the people they ruled. Among the three men, Shun was the most virtuous one. He was the son of an evil father (a court musician) and a deceitful mother.[2] His brother was arrogant but Shun could maintain peace and harmony with all of them. Imagine what kind of a good person Shun must be who could keep a harmonious relationship with an evil family.

All three men governed their people humanely. They honored affection between men and stress on honesty and sincerity. They gave first priority to emoluments rather than the exercise of power and influence. And they also let rewards went before punishments. In the Book of Rites (one of the ancient books of China), we were also told that ancient Sage-Kings practiced the five essentials to rule their world:³ 1) give eminence to men of moral excellence; 2) give eminence to men of noble positions; 3) give eminence to the old; 4) respect the elder and; 5) care for the young. Yao, Shun, and Yu diligently observed the above rites and decorum and offered reverence to heaven and their ancestors.

Although the appearance of benevolent and magnanimous emperors in ancient time was not unusual; however, the appearance of virtuous men like Yao, Shun, and Yu in a still savage world around 2500 BC at the dawn of China was amazing. How did Yao, Shun, and Yu know what virtue was? How did they develop a virtuous character to discern how to treat their fellowmen with respect and kindness? Could virtue be born to a person naturally? Could virtue be a hereditary trait pass from parents to children? All these questions are asking where did the idea of virtue come from?

Before we explore where virtue comes from, let revisit how Adam and Eve committed the original sin. It was the fruit of the knowledge of good and evil which they eaten that caused them to be ashamed of their nakedness. Before they ate the forbidden fruit, they were innocent and comfortable with their naked body. Now they saw the duality of all things-the good side and the bad side in everything. Suddenly, they acquired the knowledge of reasoning, criticism, and judgment. Suddenly, they were empowered to distinguish what are good and evil, beauty and ugly, dignity and shame. From that day onwards, human nature had degraded from pristine innocence to wise and cunning for selfish purposes.

Mengzi (Mencius), the great Confucius philosopher (370 BC to 300 BC), said human nature was innately good but circumstances could change the person from good to bad. The consequence of the original sin had corrupted the innate goodness of man and made man susceptible to do evil things in all kinds of circumstances for the benefit of the self.

The innate goodness that Mengzi talked about is the original purity of human nature which Adam and Eve had before they ate the forbidden fruit. Everyone still possesses this innate goodness in our heart. It is always there. But our innate goodness is blocked by the knowledge of good and evil which focus on the desire of the self. When under pressure, a normally good person can choose the wrong decision or do the wrong thing to satisfy his or her own selfish desire. This is the effect of original sin that corrupted human nature.

Original sin had also caused biochemical and neural imbalances in the human brain. Adam and Eve's state of mind shifted from one perspective to another instantly after they ate the forbidden fruit. They were ashamed of their nakedness immediately. The substances in the forbidden fruit must have triggered an immediate biochemical and neural reaction in their brain which awaken them to a higher level of consciousness and made them saw their nakedness in shame.

I don't know if the disobeying act of eating the forbidden fruit would be the only thing that mattered to transform Adam and Eve into a wiser and cunning human being; or if it also required the ingredients in the forbidden fruit to act as biochemical and neural catalyst to trigger the transformation. Of course, I am speculating here and there is no scientific basis whatsoever in my opinion. Nonetheless, their act of disobedience had scarred the human race with the disease of the original sin.

Nowadays, medical scientists verified many serious criminal and homosexual behaviors are caused by biochemical and neural disorder.[5] People who committed serious crime and people who propelled to abnormal sexual orientation might not know what they were doing. This may sounds ridiculous to some Christians who believe good and bad is a choice. Whether you agree or not to such causes of crime and homosexuality is up to you; however, from my Christian standpoint, this is evidence and manifestation of the disease of the original sin.

After the Fall of Adam and Eve, the corruption of human nature manifested quickly in Cain, their firstborn son born outside in to the east of Eden. Cain chose to murder his brother Abel out of jealousy that God loves Abel more than him. God gave Adam and Eve another son, Seth, to replace Abel. Seth proved to be a very virtuous man who walked in absolute righteousness under the guidance of God. Seth was chosen to be the designated forefather of the divine line where the Messiah would be born from his descendants.

In Book 1 of "The Antiquities of the Jews", Flavius Josephus, the Jewish historian who lived in A.D. 37-100, recorded that Seth was brought up as a virtuous man. Josephus said Seth could discern what was good and righteous, thus, he had an excellent character of virtue. Because of his virtuous character, his children and descendants revered God as the Lord of the universe and continued to have entire regard to virtue for seven generations! His descendants imitated Seth's virtuous character and lived happily together with no dissension and misfortunes till their death. Could you see the awesome power of virtue that influenced seven generations of Seth's posterity to imitate his virtuous character?

Josephus recorded that after seven generations, the descendants of Seth turned away from their forefathers' way of virtue. They became more and more wicked, most likely, under the influence of the descendants of Cain who thrived in their glamour and pleasure of civilization. The seventh generation was at the time of Methuselah. His father was Enoch who walked with God and didn't taste death. Methuselah begot Lamech at the age of 187 and Lamech begot Noah at the age of 182.

Noah's generation was the wickedest of all in the antediluvian world. This was the time where mankind was corrupted by fallen angels who took daughters of men as wives and their children became giants. Also, all kinds of unimaginable hybrids of human and creature corrupted the image of God. God destroyed all living things with the Deluge and spared only Noah, his three sons and their wives.

From Biblical perspective, the code of behavior that constituted virtue was passed down from Seth and his descendants of seven generations who imitated his virtuous character. Seth's impeccable virtuous character was of God who helped Adam and Eve to raise him up. It would be naïve to think that Seth or any person could simply develop into a virtuous person on his or her own. If that was the case, then God didn't have to destroy the sinful city of Sodom and Gomorra, imposed the ten commandments on the Israelites to govern their conduct, sent His prophets to preach repentance, and sent Jesus to offer His plan of salvation to mankind.

It was God who taught Seth the way of virtue and righteousness. That was how Seth learnt to be a virtuous man. Virtue has to be taught before a person can discern what is right and wrong. And virtue comes from God.

Emperor Yao, Shun and Yu were like Seth. Their exceptional virtuous character had profoundly impacted the people they ruled. They were revered as the paragon of virtuous man in ancient China. They practiced virtue with utmost devotion like Seth did. But could they develop virtuous character on their own?

If Seth was taught by God to be a virtuous man and the Israelites were taught to be godly people by the ten commandments, then there had to be someone or some people who had influenced and inspired Yao, Shun, and Yu to pursue virtue, love and kindness for others as their personal motto. Who would those people be?

Could those people be the children and descendants from the line of Shem who had migrated to China? They were the only believers of Yahweh who carried the faith of a loving and righteous God to wherever they went. They were the ones who spread the stories of the early events in the Book of Genesis in China. The stories of the virtue of Seth and the ten commandments would be inspiring messages to early Chinese people. Perhaps this was how Yao, Shun, and Yu got inspired and motivated to pursue virtue in their time when Confucius and Lao Tse were yet to be born.

It is interesting to see the earliest three dynasties of China: Xia, Shang, and Zhou each advocated one main theme in their governance of people. The Xia promoted virtue and humane treatment of people. The Shang promoted the obedience of the mandate of heaven from the Supreme God, Shang-Ti. And the Zhou promoted rites and decorum to regulate the character of Emperor and common people towards goodness. All three dynasties miraculously produced virtuous men with noble ideas for the betterment of human life without the influence of religion. From the mysterious appearance of sage kings to the emergence of a handful of benevolent emperors, I questioned if China was a land of self-made miracles?

The believers of Yahweh from the line of Shem were in pre-dynastic China. Their faith had impacted the lives of early Chinese people. Although their faith hadn't been universally adopted by all people, however, their teachings of virtue, love, and the existence of a supreme heavenly emperor, heaven, and God's will in term of mandate of heaven were accepted by rulers of many tribes and clans. This was how early Chinese people mysteriously perceived the West as the place of utopia and learnt the idea of monotheism in the form of Shang-Ti. Yao, Shun, and Yu were influenced by the faith spread by the children and descendants from the line of Shem. Although they hadn't been fully converted as believers of Yahweh, however, they were fully believers and practitioners of virtue and love of their faith.

Original sin had corrupted human nature. Virtue couldn't be an innate knowledge of man. No one can be born a virtuous person and a good person. Virtue has to be taught. God taught Seth and the Israelites to be a virtuous person. Jesus taught the apostles unconditional love and forgiveness. Therefore, Yao, Shun, and Yu couldn't self-taught themselves to be a virtuous man. God blessed Yao, Shun, and Yu to be impacted by the men of faith from the line of Shem who had migrated to China. They were the messengers and inspiration of God to help early China produced virtuous men.

CHAPTER 12 – SHANG FROM SHEM

THE CONCEPT OF MONOTHEISM was born in the ancient Near East. There is no other place on earth where monotheism thrives vehemently and passionately than this part of the world. Three great monotheistic religions: Christianity, Judaism, Islam arose and spread outward to the world from the land of the Bible.

Beginning with the Hebrew God "Yahweh", the one and only God who created the universe and mankind, monotheism ignited the world by storm. Yahweh has no name and He doesn't need one. The name Yahweh means "He is", "He causes to be", or "He brings into existence". In Hebrew, it is written as YHWH. Yahweh is a reference to this Supreme God who is the cause of all existence. Indeed God of the Bible is the Supreme Being who created everything.

Since the expulsion of Adam and Eve from Eden, Yahweh became a small candle flickering in the midst of a dark and evil world. The perversion of mankind began after Adam and Eve expulsion from Eden. The first murder happened quickly. Thereafter, sins and rebellion against God spread like contagious disease. The ancient world was infested with all kinds of idols worshipping, ancestral worshipping, superstitious beliefs, shamanism, animism, witchcraft, ghost and demonic channeling.

In China from prehistoric time to the Xia Dynasty, early Chinese people had no idea of who Yahweh was. They turned to the sun, moon, stars, mountains, rivers, and the heating of turtle shells and bones for divine inspiration and guidance. From the dawn of China to the era of Yellow Emperor, early proto-Chinese believed there were only ghosts, ancestral spirits, and demons in the spiritual realm.

Mysteriously, a people called the Shang arose to prominence in northeastern China along the Yellow River. At first, they were an influential clan to the Xia people who ruled them. They were different from other people because they believed a supreme deity called Shang-Ti who ruled heaven and earth. After being a subject of Xia Dynasty for 470 years (2070 BC - 1600 BC), they overthrown the last and ruthless Xia Emperor to incept their own Shang Dynasty.

The founder of the Shang Dynasty was Tang. He came from the Royal line of Yellow Emperor. His father, Xie, was one of the sons of Di Ku (son of his second wife) who was a grandson of Yellow Emperor. Di Ku succeeded Xia Emperor Zhuanxu (2514-2437 BC) to become Xia Emperor Di Ku (2436-2367 BC).

Tang's father, Xie, was bestowed the land of Shang in Bo in Henan province for helping Yu (later became the founder of Xia Dynasty) to tackle the flood problem. In Bo, the House of Shang was firmly established.

The House of Shang was a loyal and influential clan to the Xia dynasty for four hundreds and seventy years until the reign of the last Xia Emperor, Jie. He was an atrocious, immoral and evil emperor. Recorded in the Book of History or the Book of Document (the oldest ancient Chinese record) was an emotional speech by Tang; he told his people he was ordered by Shang-Ti to overthrow Jie. Tang said he feared not to disobey Shang-Ti and warned his people that they would be punished if they didn't help him to dethrone Jie.

After Tang killed Jie he returned to Bo, home of the House of Shang. With a show of humility Tang asked his subjects to choose a capable and benevolent person as the new Emperor. Not surprising, his people chose him to be the new emperor and he named his new dynasty the Shang Dynasty.

The origin of the Shang people was unknown. The ancestors of the Shang people were anonymous nomads that wandered into northern China in pre-dynastic time. They were nomads from outside of China because they carried a belief that was uncommon in the superstitious world of the East.

They believed in a supreme deity called "Shang-Ti" whom they believed was the heavenly emperor of heaven and earth.

The Shang people revered Shang-Ti above all gods, ghosts, and ancestral spirits. They were a god fearing people and dared not disobey Shang-Ti. Their leader, Tang, was definitely a god fearing man. He demonstrated utmost obedience to Shang-Ti equal to the patriarchs named in the genealogical line of Shem in Genesis 11:10-26. In his rally speech to his people against the last Xia emperor, Tang said he dared not to disobey Shang-Ti who ordered him to overthrow the Xia Dynasty. Tang confession of his fear of Shang-Ti won unanimous support of his Shang-Ti fearing people. Tang had shown himself to be a god fearing patriarch alike the patriarchs in the line of Shem.

How did Tang and his Shang people invent Shang-Ti without any original religion started by them? It seemed the Shang people showed up one day and Shang-Ti was already with them. Shang-Ti had to be an ancestral god whom the Shang people embraced in their family tradition.

What people in ancient time first worshipped a supreme god as their family god? There were no people other than the Israelites who professed a steadfast faith in Yahweh all their life. They were descendants from the line of Shem who was chosen to succeed the line of Seth as the divine line for the coming of the Messiah. Children and descendants from the line of Shem embraced the God of the Bible as their family God.

By their monotheistic faith, the Shang ancestors would come from the ancient Near East where monotheism originated. This region of the world was where the God of the Bible created Adam and Eve, Garden of Eden, and had spent so much time interacting with mankind and admonishing them to live in righteous way. The ancestor of the Shang people worshipped Shang-Ti like the Israelites worshipped God of the Bible. And their faith passed on to their descendant generation after generation. The Shang people were descendants from the line of Shem who had migrated to China.

The Shang people didn't invent Shang-Ti. Shang-Ti was their ancestral god. Like the Israelites in ancient Near East, the calling of their supreme deity without a name by the Shang people was strange but profound. Without a personalized name, Shang-Ti like Yahweh became a powerful and almighty god whom no one could challenge his existence. How could the Shang people invent such a grand idea to out-god their friends and foes in the superstitious savage land of ancient China? How could monotheism be born out of one people with no history of deep rooted religion? The answer is the Shang people inherited their belief from their ancestor! And who else would be their ancestor if they weren't from the line of Shem?

The pronunciation of Shang and Shem and Ham and Han caught my attention while I read the book "Legend: The Genesis of Civilization" by David Rohl, Britain's prominent Egyptologist. David discovered many archaic names of gods, places, and people had been distorted due to language variation while he was looking for clues to locate the Garden of Eden. Amazingly, by tracing the distortion of archaic name of places, David could infer and pinpoint the location of Garden of Eden and its four rivers as recorded in the Bible.

To illustrate the distortion of name due to language variation, take at look at the following archaic names and their distorted names:

Edin(Sumerian) ➡ Edinu(Akkadian) ➡ Eden(Hebrew)

Gaihun(Old Persian) ➡ Jichon(later Persian) ➡ Gihon(Hebrew)

Uizhun(Old Persian) ➡ Uzun(Iranian) ➡ Pishon(Hebrew)

Aratta(Sumerian) ➡ Urarta(Assyrian) ➡ Ararat(Hebrew)

Sumer(Sumerian) ➡ Shinar(Hebrew)

Shumer(Sumerian) ➡ Shemer ➡ Shem(Hebrew) ➡ Shang(商)

From the above table the original archaic names had been replaced by a new name due to language changes. If the above names were the name of an ancestor, the original name would be remembered and pronounced differently by his posterity after many generations. If the language distortion happened a few times, the original name would change into an entirely new name!

Indo-European language is the perfect example of language diversion from their original root language into different sub-languages. Linguists could trace the root of some of the words among the Indo-European people and the names of their common forefathers and gods who appeared in different names and pronunciations. Could such name distortion happen to the name of Shem to become Shang in ancient China?

In standard Hebrew, the name Shem is Šem; in Greek it is Sēm and; in English is Shem. All three pronounce more or less as *Sham*. In Mandarin and Cantonese Chinese, Shem is pronounced almost equally as "Sheung" with the Cantonese in a flatter tone. *Sham* and *Sheung* sound close although I could be way off in my unprofessional linguistic analysis.

In Chinese Bible, Shem is translated in the Chinese character of "Shim". This is because Shem can be pronounced as Shim in English. The translation from Hebrew to English then to Chinese could cause pronunciation distortion like the effect of the Tower of Babel on languages. My notion that the name of Shem was distorted and became Shang might sound crazy; but if we consider what happened after the Tower of Babel, how could we rule out the name of Shem had changed to Shang in China? The punishment of Tower of Babel caused the first universal language of mankind divided into thousands of languages. The name of Shem could be called many ways. What if the descendants of the Shang people remembered their remote forefather Shem as Shang in their new language after the Tower of Babel?

The earliest form of Chinese writing was the shell-bone scripts or the oracle bone script (甲骨文) inscribed on turtle plastrons or scapulas of oxen used by the Shang people for oracle reading. Whatever the Shang language was, it was certainly not Cantonese, Mandarin or Hakka Chinese. The Chinese didn't adopt a universal form of writing system until Shih-Huang-Ti of Qin Dynasty united China 901 years after the end of Shang dynasty.

Chinese character was a genius invention. There are more than 9,353 characters according to a book published in the Han Dynasty and approximately 50,000 characters in 42 books published in the Qing Dynasty. Each character is constructed to express as accurate as possible each meaning by stand alone or a combination of ideogram, pictogram, borrowed words and phonetic sound.

The construction of the Chinese character depends on the message of its creator wanted to convey. A Chinese character can be a story, picture, or meaning oriented word. The structure of the character is constructed to show the story, picture, or meaning exactly and accurately as it intended. Amazingly, some Chinese characters were found to contain hidden Bible stories!

Take a look at the Chinese character for the clan name of the Shang people: 商. This character actually depicts the Ark of Noah. The top part of this character is 立 which is commonly used to denote the roof of a house or a structure. 立 represents the shape of the roof of the Ark. Below 立 is 冂; 冂 represents the outer walls of the Ark which is rectangular like structure. Together, 立 and 冂 represents the front view of the Ark.

Inside 冂 the symbol 八 is positioned above the symbol 口. The symbol 八 denotes the number eight. The meaning of 口 is mouth. Together, it means eight mouths which is another way of Chinese expression to denote eight people. There are eight people inside the Ark.

The whole character 商 describes the Ark of Noah carrying eight survivors inside: Noah, Shem, Ham, Japheth and their four wives. What a coincidence that the Shang people chose to be represented by such an ideogram in Chinese character. Is the Chinese character 商 tells the actual memory of the Deluge? Is the character 商 telling us Shem, their remote ancestor of the Shang people, was one of the eight survivors inside the Ark?

There will be people arguing my interpretation of the character 商. Some Chinese linguists interpreted 商 meaning eight people negotiating business deals in some sort of a trading house. I respect their interpretation but I wonder why it needs eight people to do business negotiation? Why not two or four people? The selection of eight people in 商 is rather unusual because there is no mandatory law in ancient China that you must have eight people to conduct business negotiation. So why did the creator of 商 insert eight people inside the structure of his word?

Furthermore, it is very strange that Chinese people chose the number eight to denote growth, success, and prosperity. Why did the Chinese pick the number eight as the divine number of prosperity? Could it be originated from the idea of the blessing of the repopulation of the world by Noah and his family? What other number could exalt the sacred blessing of prosperity on mankind better than number eight?

Eight is the divine number to the Chinese. This was why China chose August 8, 2008 (8-8-8) as the opening date for the Summer Olympic Games in

Beijing. The eight survivors in the story of the Ark of Noah were sacred number to the ancestors of the Shang people. They were the ones who spread the divinity of number eight to all Chinese people.

Ancient people passed down stories to their descendants to keep their people's legacy alive. But memories passed in such way became vague and distorted over time. After a long time, these stories can only be remembered as myths and legends in bits and pieces of obscured truth. Memory of the Shang people's remote ancestor was gradually forgotten after they were isolated in ancient China from their biblical homeland for hundreds of years. Many of their descendants had mixed with other people who believed in other superstitions. Finally, the fate of their biblical heritage and belief ended in oblivion in China.

Shang-Ti and the clan name of Shang were evidences left behind by the descendants from the line of Shem who had migrated to pre-dynastic China. The migrated descendant of Shem emerged as Shang people in early china. After the Tower of Babel, they still worshipped Yahweh as Shang-Ti whom they called in their new language. Shang Dynasty had her glorious time like the Kingdom of Israel under King David and King Solomon. Shang Dynasty lasted 716 years (1766 to 1050 BC) in China until they were overthrown by the Zhou people who incepted the Zhou Dynasty.

CHAPTER 13 – HAN FROM HAM

HAN (漢) IS THE CLAN NAME of Chinese people who regard themselves as the pure Chinese race. Of all the 56 ethnic groups in present day China, the Han people compose an overwhelming 93% of the population.

The origin of the Han people is unknown. However, the Hans traced their remote ancestor to Yellow Emperor and Yan Emperor (Emperor Shennong who was also called the "Flame Emperor"). From these two mythical emperors, the Hans also called themselves the Huaxia people, the descendants of Yellow Emperor and Yan Emperor.

The Chinese character "Han" (漢) depicts water denoted by three strokes to describe a river on the left side and joined by the other half of the character 莫 on the right which means toil and hardship. The Han character suggests the ancestor of the Han people lived by the river where their livelihood would likely be fishing. However, the character Han might have a deeper and symbolic message of hardship related to disaster of water. Could it be a devastating flood where ancestors of the Han people had struggled with?

Ancient Chinese records mentioned there was a State of Han under the Qin rule, but there was no detail of the people living there. Also mentioned was the Han River, a principal tributary of the Yangtze River (Chang Jiang). It has a total length of about 950 miles (1,530 km). It rises in the mountains in southwestern Shaanxi and becomes the Han River at Hanzhong and flows through a fertile basin some 60 miles (100 km) long and 12 miles (19 km) wide; then cuts through a series of deep gorges and emerges into the central Yangtze basin in Hubei province. Is this the river which the character of Han is describing?

No one knows if the Han River has anything to do with the origin of the Han people. I supposed the Han River being so named would more or less relate to the people inhabited around there. Perhaps the ancestor of the Han people lived there in the beginning when they first arrived in China. Perhaps the Han River was named for historical event happened there. No one knows for certain.

In South Korea, there is also a Han River by that name which once been used as a trade route to China. But now it is no longer in used because of its geographic location between the sensitive border of North and South Korea. The Han River in Korea was named by the Korean people who had close cultural ties with China since ancient time.

I have researched many Chinese history books but couldn't find the origin of the Han people in ancient China. I could only find a people called "Hon" in the Spring and Autumn period (a period prior to the unification of the China by Emperor Shih-Huang-Ti). The Hon people were descendants of King Wen of the Zhou Dynasty. Their leader's name was Wu Zi but he changed his surname from Ji to Hon when he was offered the city of Han Yuan.

Why did Wu Zi changed his surname to Hon was unknown. Surname was an honor to ancient Chinese people. Chinese surname is like a brand name and tells people where a person heritage comes from. Perhaps Wu Zi changed his surname in order to claim the possession of the city of Han Yuan; or perhaps he wanted to reinstate the name of his ancestor where his heritage derived.

The character "Hon" is also the racial name of the Korean people. Chinese people called the Korean people the Hon people. The Chinese character for Hon (韓) is an entirely different character from the character Han (漢). The pronunciation of "Hon" and "Han" sound close with the latter end in a slightly higher tone.

Whether the forefather of the Korean people had any ancestral link with the Hon people of Wu Zi was unknown. I am open to the possibility that some descendants of the Korean Hon people had migrated to China from the Korean peninsula and became part of the Han Chinese. The Hon people of Korea were the closest people I could find who might have clan connection with the Han people.

The Hans were not a prominent people until the inception of the Han Dynasty. The Han Dynasty was incepted in 202 BC and lasted 433 years till 221 AD. The rise of the Han people was dramatic. In the ending period of the Qin Dynasty (209 BC), two peasants by the name of Chen Sheng (also known as Chen She) and Wu Guang (also known as Wu Shu) successfully incited and started a revolt against the Qin Emperor. Many peasants joined them in their course to overthrow the Qin regime. Unfortunately, Chen and Wu died before they saw their dream came true.

After them emerged two dynamic leaders to lead the revolt against the Qin. They were Xiang Yu and Liu Bang. Xiang Yu was of noble decent and Liu Bang was of peasant class. Together they crumbled the Qin Empire but immediately entered into rivalry against each other for who should be the next Emperor of China. In the end Liu Bang defeated Xiang Yu and rose to power to become Emperor Gaodi, the first emperor of the Han Dynasty.

Liu Bang came from a humble background in the peasant class in the Peixian County in modern Jiangsu Province. In the beginning of his rivalry with Xiang Yu for the supremacy of China, he was defeated by Xiang Yu and forced to accept the title of "Han Wang" (The Prince of Han) and retreat his army to a place called Ba-shu (Yizhou). The title of "Han Wang" bestowed to Liu Bang by Xiang Yu indicated that Li's heritage might be of the Han clan. If so, Han must be a clan name of the Han people despite of their obscure origin.

The Han Empire was the mightiest dynasty in China that could rival the Roman Empire in the West in their time. The Han army was also fierce fighting men led by valiant generals to protect Han China from the barbarians. At one point in time, the Han army had conquered and controlled all the territory leading to Central Asia in the West and established many vassal states and alliances for Han China. If the Han army marched on farther west, they would surely encounter the Roman soldiers stationed in Asia Minor.

Bible scholars suggested that Sini, one of the twelve sons of Canaan who founded the Sinite nation, was the biblical forefather of the Chinese.[2] Thus, the Latin prefix "Sino" was derived from Sini which denoted things related to China.[3] For example, Sinology is the study of China; Sino-US trade denotes the economic activities between China and the US and so forth. Furthermore, Chinese surname such as "Sin", "Siang", and "Ch'in (or Qin)" is thought to be derived from "Sin".

Quoting Isaac 49:12: "*Surely these shall come from afar; Look, those from the north and the west; And these from the <u>land of Sinim</u>.*" Some Bible scholars see "Sinim" to be a direct reference to China in ancient time. However, other Bible scholars argue that Sinim refers to Syene (Aswan) in Egypt and not in China. However, the verse in Isaac 49:12 emphasizes that Sinim was a far away place ("*Surely these shall come from afar…*). How could Sinim be in Egypt? Egypt was not a distant land to the Israelites. Egypt was a neighboring nation within reachable distance and the Israelites had close encounters with the Egyptians all the time. Clearly, those Bible scholars who see Sinim in Egypt might have overlooked the emphasis of far away land in Isaac 49:12.

No body knew what happened to the Sinites. They seemed to have disappeared from ancient Mesopotamia and moved to distant land. Could it be China where the Sinites restarted their new life? If so, many Sinites fled to China probably after the curse of Noah in Genesis 9:24 which stirred the exodus of Canaanites to other lands. Noah's cursed the Canaanites would be slaves to the Shemites and Japhethites. If I were a Canaanite, I would flee as far as I could away from the Shemites and Japhethites. Who want to be a slave and who want their children to be slaves? The curse of Noah aroused many Canaanites including the Sinites-probably large number of them-to move far away.

If the Sinites moved and settled in China, they would proudly proclaimed their heritage from the line of Ham where their most renowned forefathers was Nimrod, the mightiest hunter in the eyes of the Lord. But the Sinites were very quiet and in very low profile much like the Han people who nobody knew until Liu incepted the Han Dynasty.

The name "Sin" was also the name of a moon god in Mesopotamian mythology.4 The original name of Sin was called "Nanna" and "Suen". Sin was the Akkadian pronunciation of Suen. The descendants of the Sinites were moon worshippers and Sin was their principal god. The religion of Sin wasn't a prominent religion in Mesopotamia because the Sinites weren't a prominent people unlike their other brothers who were renowned people: Sidonites, Hittites, Jebusites, Amorites, Girgashites, Hivites, Arvadites, Zemarites, and Hamathites.

Chinese people celebrate the moon festival once a year. Chinese legend tells a story of an archer named "Shen Yi" and his wife "Heng-O". Shen earned the elixir of immortality from the gods. However, while he was out on business, the elixir was accidentally swallowed by his wife. She fled and was pursued by an angry Yi. She escaped by floating up to the Moon and stayed there forever. Later Shen forgave her and built her a palace on the moon and visit her once a month. The story was about love and reunion to encourage Chinese family gets together once a year under a full moon in the fall season. The moon festival in China isn't related to any religion but for whatever reason, Chinese people adore the moon.

The Han people were not a believer of a supreme god. Unlike the Shang people who worshiped a Supreme Deity called Shang-Ti as their ancestral god, the Han people had no such religious loyalty to one or any god(s). The Han people adopted and practiced Confucianism which emphasized on human effort rather than depending on a supreme god or gods. Taoism was also popular during the Han Dynasty but it had nothing to do with any particular god or gods. The Han people never pursue the idea of monotheism like the Shang people. If the Han people were originated from the line of Ham, they would be rebellious against any supreme god who endorsed the curse of Noah upon their descendants to be slaves of anyone.

The descendants from the line of Ham produced mighty warrior and civilization. One of Ham's sons, Mizraim, went to Egypt and his descendants found the magnificent civilization of Egypt. Nimrod, one of the seven sons of Cush (grandson of Ham), went to Babylon and became a mighty warrior and ruler of all people in his time. Nimrod incited all people in his world to build a tower to reach heaven. We all know what happened to this lofty endeavor which led to the division and scatter of mankind by language by God.

The Han people also produced a number of great emperors and great generals who advanced the territory of the Han Empire all the way to Central

Asia. At the zenith of Han Dynasty, the Hans extended their empire to Central Asia beyond the Taklimakan Desert in the west, to Tibet in the southwest, and to Manchuria (Korea) in the northeast. The Han army defeated their long time barbaric enemy, Xiongnu, and drove them farther away to the West. The glory and power of Han Dynasty rivaled that of the Roman Empire in the West.

The descendants of Canaan spread throughout the Mediterranean and emerged as great people such as the Phoenician, Philistine, Amorite, and Hittite. The Canaanites were great warriors and so were the Han people. The trait of Nimrod mighty warrior's blood was in the Han people. Han people too had become a mighty people and made Han China a superpower in ancient East Asia. They were definitely a people of great warriors that could rival any great army in their time.

Ancient Chinese surnames were derived from the name of their ancestor more than any other sources. If the Han people claimed their clan name from their remote ancestor, who would assume to be their forefather better than Ham, one of the three progenitors of mankind after the Deluge. The name "Han" could be the eponym of the name "Ham" after the event of the Tower of Babel. Like the name "Shang" which could be distorted to "Shem" in the new language spoken by the early Chinese. Ham could be the remote forefather of the Han people whom they had forgotten after isolated and struggled in China for a very long period of time.

The Han people were a great people in China. Their descendants propagated the largest number of population in China. The Han's culture is the dominant heritage of the Chinese people. Their emergence as China's elite race is no accident.

CHAPTER 14 – CAUCASIANS FROM JAPHETH

JAPHETH HAD SEVEN SONS: Gomer, Magog, Madai, Javan, Tubal, Meshech, and Tiras. His descendants were mostly identified as the ancestors of European Caucasian people that spread to Europe, Russia, and northern India.

Noah blessed Japheth that God would extend his territory and that he would share his blessings with Shem. The European descendants of Japheth turned out to be amazing conquerors and adventurers extending their outreach for land far beyond their imagination. From Alexander the Great, European Caucasians spread out and conquered many lands in the world. The legacy of their expansions can still be seen today in Hong Kong, Macau, Singapore, Malaysia, Australia, New Zealand, India, Africa, and even America and Canada. God indeed extended Japheth descendant's territories enormously.

In the East, Japheth's European descendants had left their footprints in the western border of China as early as 4,000 years ago. European mummies unearthed in the arid foothills of the Tian Shan ("Celestial Mountain") in northwest China and the fringes of the Taklimakan Desert in Xinjiang shocked historians by their arrival in China much earlier than expected. The implication of the European mummies unearthed in this part of China meant that ancient Europeans had entered China and might have mingled with early Chinese people.

Traditionally, Bible scholars see Japheth descendants as the ancestors of European Caucasian people such as the Greek, Roman, Gaul, Irish, Welsh, and other northern Europeans.[1] But one of Japheth sons might turn out to be the ancestor of an Asiatic race. He was the well known Magog that Bible scholars identified as the ancestor of the Scythians that thrived in the Eurasia Steppe. Bible scholars also see Magog associated with the Russian people who will be a key player in Armageddon in the end time.

During my research, I came across an anonymous author of a book called "In Search of the Origin of Nations".[2] The author presents an interesting proposition but may not be a popular one to western Bible scholars. He explained that the name "Mongol" was derived from Japheth's son "Magog". From the word Mongol derived the term "Mongoloid" which was used to refer to Asiatic people with slit eyes, straight hairs, and fair to yellow skin. There are also names equal to Mongol such as Moghul called by the East Indian and Majuj (who were the Scythian) called by the Arabs; both are derived from the name "Magog". It is a refreshing proposition by the author of the above book. And it could be a new revelation to the origin of the Mongoloids where I would research more for my future writings. I believe the distortion of the name "Magog" to so many versions was the result of language division after the Tower of Babel.

The above proposition that Chinese people were descended from the line of Magog might not be far fetched even though most Biblical scholars would shake their head. According to Flavius Josephus, the Jewish historian (37 AD - 100 AD) who wrote "The Antiquities of The Jews", the descendants of Magog became the Scythian that thrived across the Eurasia steppes to Mongolia. To the West they were called Scythian but in the East they were called Yueh-Chi, Xiongnu, and Mongol by the Chinese.

Both East and West Scythians were regarded as obnoxious barbarians by the civilized nations that they intruded, raid and pillaged relentlessly. As said in the chapter "Tower of Babel", I believe many new groups, tribes, nations, or whatever you called it became a heterogeneous people of Mongoloid, Caucasian, and Negro. They were forced to group together by language so that they could understand each other. Therefore, the Scythians could be a people of Mongoloids, Caucasians, and Negroes just like any other newly formed language groups of mixed people after the Tower of Babel. This was the reason why ancient nomads across the Eurasia Steppes were sometime depicted as Caucasians and sometime as Mongoloids. Ancient Chinese historical documents recorded that the

Mongols had color eyes and hairs. This had to be evidence of mixed race between Caucasian and Mongoloid Scythians.

The Scythians strived in riding horses, thus they were perfect nomads to roam all over the Eurasian Steppe. As their number and tribe increased, I believed the Scythians split into two people with the Caucasian Scythians concentrated in the West and the Mongoloid Scythians concentrated in the East. The split could be the result of the people they fought and mingled with where the Caucasians thrived mainly in the west and the Mongoloids mainly in the east.

The unification of all Mongol tribes by Genghis Khan enabled this large army of fierce warriors to invade and inflict unimaginable horrible and devastating calamities over many nations across Eurasia. From China to Eastern Europe, the Mongols were seen as the devils from hell. No Asiatic race had conquered so many lands from Asia to Europe than the Mongol in the entire history of mankind. If the Mongols were from the line of Magog, the blessing of extending territories to the Japhethites also came through to this fearsome people of the East.

Although the Mongol and the Chinese were both Mongoloid type of people, however their cultures were like two sharp edges. The Mongols were no match to the superior civilized Chinese people. It must be God's will that the barbaric Mongols subdued the Chinese so that they could be civilized. The Mongols led by Genghis Khan conquered China and ruled the Chinese under the Yuan Dynasty from 1279 AD to 1368 AD. The irony of the Mongol Dynasty was that the Mongolians had assimilated into the Chinese culture instead of the other way around. The Mongols adopted the Chinese way of life and became more Chinese themselves. Two hundreds and seventy six years later when the Manchurians conquered and incepted the Qing Dynasty, they too repeated the experience of the Mongols and became more Chinese than their own race. The advanced culture of the Chinese was too hot for barbarians not to appreciate and possess to be their own!

Whether the Mongol was from one of the lines of Magog or not, God had blessed Japheth's descendant tremendous success in their quest for new territories. The discovery of ancient European mummies in the border of western China is evidence that early people settled in China were not just Mongoloids alone. Caucasian and Negro people were there despite of their minority status; they were there and they might have synergized with the Mongoloid Chinese people in the rise of Chinese civilization.

CHAPTER 15 - CHINESE CHARACTERS

The earliest form of Chinese characters was the shell-bone scripts or the oracle bone script (甲骨文) inscribed on turtle plastrons or scapulas of oxen. They were used by the Shang people for oracle reading. The shell-bone script characters are symbols more than picture. Over the course of time from the Zhou Dynasty to the Han Dynasty, Chinese characters had evolved into a proficient and stylish form of writing and employed pictogram, phonetic sound, abstract idea, borrowed meaning, and calligraphic styles to convey messages.

Chinese character is a one-syllable word, thus, Chinese writing is termed morpheme-syllabic script. Since Han Dynasty, the Han's characters became the formal Chinese writing for all Chinese. In modern mainland China, a simplified version of Chinese characters (简体字) has replaced the traditional version of Chinese character (繁體字) where it is still use in Taiwan and Hong Kong.

Although Chinese characters had evolved from their earliest form throughout the history of China, however, the construction of Chinese character differs word by word. The original creator of each Chinese character must have endeavored to construct and convey the message of each word clearly, thus, they would either rely on their creative imagination or memories of events that they recalled to represent the message of the character. It is not easy to comprehend the brilliance behind the construction of the Chinese characters. However, one thing is clear; every Chinese character is constructed to convey its message as accurately as possible, therefore, Chinese character employs whatever means (symbol, phonetic, borrow meaning, and pictogram) necessary to construct the character. The meticulous construction of the Chinese character means that each character can represents a message, image, story or historical event its creator wants to tell. It is truly remarkable and ingenious.

Some years ago I came across a book called *"The Discovery of Genesis with the subtitle: How the truth of Genesis were found hidden in the Chinese language"* published by Concordia Publishing House in St. Louis, Missouri, USA in 1979. It is written by Reverend C.H. Kang and Dr. Ethel R. Nelson. In the book Kang dissected Chinese characters which seemed to tell the stories in the early chapters of Genesis. This is a small book which could be read through in an hour.

I selected to comment on some of the following Chinese characters that seemed to tell the stories in the early chapters in the Book of Genesis for your reference. I highly recommended readers interested in learning more about the biblical implication of certain unique Chinese characters to read the above book by Reverend C.H. Kang and Dr. Ethel R. Nelson.

裸

This character means "naked". The left part of the character 裸 represents clothing and the right part 果 represents fruit. On top of 果 is another character 田 which represents field or garden and the lower part of 果 is another character 木 which represents wood or forest.

The creator of this character seems to convey a picture of a garden of trees or forest where no clothing is needed. The Bible tells us God created Adam and Eve naked and put them in the Garden of Eden to enjoy their lives. What are the chances the creator of this character possesses knowledge of the Garden of Eden in the making of this character?

魔

This is the character represents the Devil. Inside 魔, on the top is the character 林 which represents the word for forest and on the bottom the character 鬼 represents the word for ghost. Why did the creator of this character put a ghost in a forest to represent the Devil? Shouldn't the image of a terrified beast be more appropriate to convey the image of the Devil? Instead, the creator of this character chose to put a ghost in a forest to tell us the Devil is in the forest. The Bible tells us the Devil first appeared as a slick serpent tempting Eve in the forest inside the Garden of Eden. Who told the creator of this character the first temptation of mankind by the Devil in the Garden of Eden?

苦

This character means "sorrow", "bitter", or "suffering". In Genesis 3:17-18 God cursed Adam and Eve to toil and eat herbs from the ground in sorrow and sweat for the rest of their lives after they committed the original sin. The top part of this character is like two joined crosses which denote plants and weeds. The bottom part 古 is the character for "ancient". If we split 古 into half, we come up with two characters: 十 (character for number "10") on the top and 口 (character for "mouth") on the bottom. The character 十 denotes ten fingers used for picking up and putting food into 口 which represents the mouth.

    Putting it back together, the character 苦 describes God punishment to Adam and Eve for the original sin. From that cursed day onwards, they had to toil with two hands for labor and food. Before they committed the original sin, Adam and Eve enjoyed a perfect existence in a utopia where fruits are everywhere and whenever they want. What a great sorrow it must be for mankind to lose the blessed privileges of a wonderful and effortless life. The creator of this character chose labor in toil to convey the message of sorrow rather than using death. This character wants to tell us the greatest sorrow of mankind is the lost privilege of Eden where life is perfect and abundance without hardship.

This character means "flood". The left side of the character consists of three strokes denote water. The right side 共 is the character meaning total or together. The top part of 共 is a structure and the bottom part is 八 which is the character for number "eight". The creator of this character seemed to tell us a total of eight people inside a structure in a flood. This was the story of Noah, his three sons and their wives inside the Ark.

This is the character for vessel, ship or boat. The left side of this character 舟 is the character for vessel. On top of the right side is the character 八 for the number 8 and on the bottom is the character 口 for the word mouth. This is another character telling the story of Noah and the Deluge. The creator of this character chose 8 to put on a vessel and didn't choose 6, 9, or any other number. Why is the number 8 so popular? Could the story of the Ark of Noah and the Deluge the basis for defining vessel to remind mankind of the first unsinkable vessel in the world?

商

The character 商 is discussed in the chapter "Shang from Shem". 商 is the name for the Shang people and the Shang Dynasty (1700-1027 BC). The origin of Shang people is unknown; however, they worshipped a supreme deity called Shang-Ti which made them likely to be the descendant from the line of Shem who had migrated and settled in the beginning time of China. In my opinion, 商 is the distorted name of Shem after the Tower of Babel.

塔

This character is the word for tall tower. The left side 土 denotes "clay". The right side 荅 denotes undertaking together under a roof. The ideogram of this character seems to convey unity in an undertaking from the ground to the roof. Could this character trying to tell us the story of the Tower of Babel?

乱

This is the word for "confusion". This character is clearly constructed out of the story of the Tower of Babel. The right side of this character ㄴ represents the leg or right leg of a man thus suggested walking or implies fleeing. The left side of the character is 舌 which is the character for tongue. The 舌 character is made up of 千 on the top and 口 on the bottom. 千 is the character for the number 1,000 and 口 is the character for mouth; Together it becomes 1,000 mouths. How did the creator of this character come up with 1,000 mouths and walking or fleeing leg to describe confusion? The 1,000 mouths must be referring to thousand or thousands of languages which caused immense confusion. What caused people to speak in 1,000 languages? The creator of this character must be referring to the event of the Tower of Babel where God scattered mankind by confusing their languages. Can there be other reason behind the construction of this character clearer than this? What are the chances the creator of this character imagines something like this to convey confusion?

    Chinese characters are works of genius. The idea behind the construction of the character had to originate from either creative imagination or memories of actual events which the creator of the character remembered, and which he or she felt would convey the best or accurate idea of the message or story that he or she wanted the character to tell.

I believe Chinese Characters had unknowingly recorded the events told in the early chapter of the Book of Genesis.

SUGGESTED TIMELINE

????? God created Adam and Eve

10000-8000 BC

- Pre-Fall Children scattered all over the world. Primitive Chinese People existed in China

- Adam & Eve expelled from Eden
- Birth of Cain and Abel
- Cain killed Abel; God replaced Abel with Seth
- Cain built 1st city

- Sage YouChao/Suiren appeared in China

- <u>Genesis 5:1-3 Genealogy of Seth to Noah</u>: Some other sons and daughters from the line of Seth reached China. Also, children from line of Cain. They were the first wave of migrants to China from the biblical land.

- Fallen Angels took daughters of men as wives. Their offspring Nephilim adored by men as mighty men and heroes

7500 BC

- The Deluge: All mankind including those in China killed.
-

After 7500 BC

- <u>Genesis 11:10-26: Genealogy of Shem to Abraham</u>: Some other sons and daughters from the line of Shem reached China. They were the second wave of migrants to China

- Sage Fu Xi, Nuwa, Shennong appeared in China

- Yangshao Culture
- Noah cursed Canaan, son of Ham
- Tower of Babel
-

2852- 2205 BC

- Yellow Emperor
- Virtuous Emperor Yao, Shun and Yu
- 2205-1766 BC? Xia Dynasty
- 1766-1122 BC Shang Dynasty
- 1122-221 BC Zhou Dynasty

GENERAL REFERENCES

CHINESE HISTORY AND ARCHAEOLOGY RELATED

The Origin of Chinese Civilization. Edited by David N. Keightley. 1983 University of California Press, California, USA

Early Chinese Civilization: Anthropological Perspectives. K.C. Chang. 1976 the Harvard-Yenching Institute (Harvard University Press), England

Northeast Asia in Prehistory. Chester S. Chard. 1974 The University of Wisconsin Press, Wisconsin, USA

The Cradle of the East: An Inquiry into the Indigenous Origins of Techniques and Ideas of Neolithic and Early Historic China, 5000-1000 B.C. Ping-Ti Ho. 1975 the Chinese University of Hong Kong

The Prehistory of China: An Archaeological Exploration. Judith M. Treistman. 1972 Doubleday & Company Inc, New York published for The American Museum of Natural History & the Natural History Press

Shang Civilization. Kwang-Chih Chang. 1980 New Haven: Yale University Press, USA

Mysteries of Ancient China: New Discoveries From the Early Dynasties. Edited by Jessica Rawson. 1996 The British Museum Press (A division of The British Museum Company Ltd.)

An Outline History of China. Bai Shouyi. 2002 Foreign Languages Press Beijing

China: An Interpretive History. Joseph R. Levenson & Franz Schurmann. 1969 The Regents of University of California Press, CA

Ancient China: Chinese Civilization From the Origins To the Tang Dynasty. Maurizio Scarpari. 2000, 2006 White Star S.p.a, Italy

China Before The Han Dynasty. William Watson. 1961 Western Printing Services Ltd, Bristol, Great Britain

Ancient China: Art and Archaeology. Jessica Rawson. 1980 The Trustees of the British Museum and published simultaneously by Fitzhenry & Whiteside Ltd, Toronto, Canada

Ancient China. Edward H. Schafer. 1967 Time Life Books, USA

The Horizon History of China. 1969 American Heritage Publishing Co. Inc., New York

Ancient China. Edward H. Schafer. 1967 Time Inc., USA

CHINESE TRADITION AND CULTURE RELATED

The Forgotten Tribes of China. Kevin Sinclair. 1987 Intercontinental Publishing Corporation Limited, Hong Kong

The Chinese Heritage: A New and Provocative View of the Origins of Chinese Society. K.C. Wu. 1982 K.C. Wu and published simultaneously by General Publishing Company Ltd in Canada

Confucianism: The Analects of Confucius. Translated by James Legge. Editor: Jaroslav Pelikan. 1992 HarperCollins Publishers, USA

Heritage of China: Contemporary Perspectives on Chinese Civilization. Edited by Paul S. Ropp. 1990 The Regents of the University of California, CA

The Chinese Heritage. K.C. Wu. 1982 Crown Publisher Inc., New York

The Book of Rites (Selections). Published by Shandong Friendship Press

An Intellectual History of China. Revised and translated by He Zhaowu. 1991 Foreign Languages Press, Beijing, China

China's Minority Nationalities. Edited by Ma Yin. 1994 Foreign Languages Press Beijing

Cultural Flow Between China and Outside World Throughout History. Shen Fuwei. 1996 Foreign Languages Press Beijing

Shu Ching (Book of History): A modernized edition of the translations of James Legge. Clae Waltham. 1971 Henry Regnery Company, Chicago, IL, USA

The Book of History (A Chinese-English Bilingual Edition). English translation by Du Ruiging. Published by Shandong Friendship Press, China

The Forgotten Tribes of China. Kevin Sinclair. 1987 Intercontinental Publishing Corporation Limited, Hong Kong

WORLD HISTORY RELATED

World Prehistory: A Brief Introduction-Fourth Edition. Brian M Fagan. 1999 Lindbriar Corporation, USA

The Royal Horde: Nomad Peoples of the Steppes. E.D. Phillips. Copyright 1965 Thames and Hudson; printed by Jarrold and Sons Ltd, Norwich, England

The First Great Civilizations: Life in Mesopotamia, the Indus Valley, and Egypt. Jacquetta Hawkes. 1973 Alfred A. Knopf Inc. New York

The Story of Civilization: 1 Our Oriental Heritage. Will Durant. First published 1935 by Simon & Schuster Inc. Recent edition by MJF Books, New York

Earliest Civilization of the Near East. James Mellaant. 1965 Thames and Hudson Ltd., London

Cradle of Civilization. Samuel Noah Kramer. 1967 Time Inc., USA

The First Cities. Dora Jane Hamblin. 1973 Time Inc., USA

OTHER

The Discovery of Genesis: How the Truths of Genesis Were Found Hidden in the Chinese language. C.H. Kang & Ethel R. Nelson. 1979 Concordia Publishing House, St. Louise

The Tarim Mummies. J.P. Mallory & Victor H. Mair. 2000 Thames & Hudson Ltd., London, England

The Genesis Record: A Scientific and Devotional Commentary on the Book of Beginnings. Henry M. Morris. 1976 Baker Books, Grand Rapids, MI

The Writing Systems of the World. Florian Coulmas. 1989 Basil Blackwell Ltd, Oxford, UK

Mysteries of the Past. Lionel Casson, Robert Claiborne, Brian Fagan, Walter Karp and edited by Joseph J. Thorndike. JR. 1977 American Heritage Publishing Co. Inc., USA

Fallen Angels and the Origins of Evil. Elizabeth Clare Prophet. 2000 Summit University Press, MT, USA

The Mummies of Ürümchi. Elizabeth Wayland Barber. 1999 W.W. Norton & Company Inc., New York

Noah's Flood. William Ryan & Walter Pitman. 1998 Touchstone 2000, New York

Legend: The Genesis of Civilization. David Rohl. 1998 The Random House Group Ltd., London

From Eden to Exile. David Rohl. 2002 Century, The Random House Group Ltd., London. First published as *The Lost Testament.*

Mapping Human History: Discovering the Past Through Our Genes. Steve Olson. 2002 Houghton Mifflin Company, New York

The Settlement of the Americas: A New Prehistory. Thomas D. Dill hay. 2000 Basic Books, New York

The Origin of Native Americans: Evidence from Anthropological Genetics. Michael H. Crawford. 1998 Cambridge University Press, United Kingdom

The Jesus Sutras. Martin Palmer. 2001 The Ballantine Publishing Group, New York and simultaneously published by The Random House of Canada Ltd, Toronto

Myths of China and Japan. Donald A. Mackenzie. 1994 Random House Value Publishing Inc., New Jersey

Chinese Mythology. Donald A. Mackenzie. 1994 Random House Value Publishing Inc., New Jersey, USA

Chinese Mythology. Anthony Christie. 1985 Peter Bedrick Books, New York

In Search of the Origin of Nations. History Research Project. 2003 Bloomington Ind.

The Works of Josephus (translated by William Whiston). Peabody, Mass.: Hendrickson, 1991, c1987.

MAGAZINE

Discover Magazine, March 1996. Uniformity: The Great Chinese puzzle P. 79-85

Discover Magazine, December 2004. The Hidden History of Men p. 32-39

Discover Magazine, April 1994. The Mummies of Xinjiang P.68-77

Archaeology Magazine, March/April 1995. Mystery Mummies of Ancient China P.29-35

National Geographic, March 2006. The Greatest Journey Ever Told: The Trail of Our DNA P.61-73